JAIL JUDGES & JUSTICE IN ANCIENT INDIA

JAIL JUDGES & JUSTICE IN ANCIENT INDIA

S. NARAIN

Forword by

Sh. S.N.P. Sinha

Chairman

Bar Council of India

Rouse Avenue, New Delhi

Book - review by

Dr S.C. Raina

Professor - Head Law Centre

University of Delhi

KALPAZ

ISBN: 978-93-5128-249-5

Price: ₹ 590

First Published, 2017

Published by

Kalpaz Publications
C-30, Satyawati Nagar,
Delhi – 110052
E-mail: kalpaz@hotmail.com
Ph.: 9212142040

Printed at: G. Print Process, Delhi

Cataloging in Publication Data—DK
Courtesy: D.K. Agencies (P) Ltd. <docinfo@dkagencies.com>

Narain, S., author.
Jail judges & justice in ancient India / S. Narain ; foreword by Sh. S.N.P. Sinha ; book-review by Dr S.C. Raina.
pages cm
ISBN 9789351282495

1. Justice, Administration of—India—History. 2. Justice, Administration of (Hindu law) I. Title. II. Title: Jail judges and justice in ancient India.

KNS3411.N37 2016 DDC 347.54 23

EMINENT JURISTS SPEAK

Shri Narayan's book is very educative. The author has given excerpts from original texts in Sanskrit and that way all ideas projected in his book are authentic and authoritative. The book is very comprehensive and compact at the same time. The historical account of Judicial system in India from Vedic period upto pre-British period as traced in the Book is interesting.

- M.N. Krishna Murti
Sr. Advodate & President
Bar Council - Supreme Court

I congratulate the author to focus in depth on the salient feature of judicial system in ancient India in different periods, beginning from Vedic age The book "Jail, Judges and Justice in Ancient India" is not only the eye opener of rich cultural heritage of Ancient India but at the same time would enlighten the Judges, Academicians and the Students who were working in different walks of life including legal profession.

- S. N. P. Sinha
Chairman
Bar Council of India

I am impressed by the whole book in general and the chapter 6 & 7 in particular. The author has structured the hierarchy of courts in ancient India and the way the courts were handling the matter and disposing off them in speedy way. Reading of the whole book makes one to think that can we in India adopt such a system for the purpose of reducing the areas in courts, making justice speedy, transparent and affordable

- S.C. Raina
Prof. in-Charge
Delhi University Law Centre

Vedas Speak

"O noble king, like a father go near thy subject, and let the subjects like sons come near thee to seek protection. Just as fire is kindled with woodsticks, so hear thy complaint and kindle justice. Let versatile, learned and noble-minded queens, like mother, hear the complaints of women, and do justice unto them!"

- Yajur Veda

Foreword

India is the heir of one of the most intellectual and spiritual based civilization of the world. But on account of the conspicuous absence of systematic research, little is known about the rich cultural heritage of India, particularly in the sphere of ancient law and justice delivery system. It is interesting to read the methods followed in ancient India as to how the proceedings of the court were conducted, how the witnesses were examined, how the defendant or accused was called upon and judgment delivered. The methodology followed to extract truth from the accused and the ordeals conducted in cases where there was no eye witness and modern kinds of narcotic tests and brain mapping were not available, is really refreshing to read.

The sincere attempt by Shri S. Narain shall bridge the long standing gap in respect of research and knowledge in this important yet neglected phase of ancient India. The judicial system in ancient India was based upon moral and social values, standard of conduct and the ancient philosophy. Merits like speedy justice transparency and affordability under ancient system can provide national reorientation to the present system.

The student of science and technology turned author of different spheres of knowledge of ancient India. Shri S. Narain who is author of' many books viz Examination in Ancient India, Doctors, Scientists & engineers of Ancient India,

Marriages Romance and Married Life in Ancient India (Ancient to Modern), Education and Examination Systems in Ancient India, Technical Education, Technical Universities and Technical Institutions of Ancient India and lastly the book "Jail, Judges and Justice in Ancient India" are the landmark achievements of retired life, the present "Jail, Judges and Justice in Ancient India" is not only the eye opener of rich cultural heritage of Ancient India but at the same time would enlightene the Judges, Academicians and the Students who were working in different walks of life including legal profession.

I congradulate the author to focus in depth on the salient feature of judicial system in ancient India in different periods, beginning from Vedic age and I am sure that the book may be useful for scholars, the judges and students in the area of law and justice.

7/11/09

(S. N. P. Sinha)
Chairman
Bar Council of India

Key Note

I glanced through Shir S. Narain's book: "Jail, Judges and Justice in Ancient india". It is an interesting research work. What is justice after all? Justice is not law. Sometimes law and justice may even conflict. But in ancient India the whole object of law was to render justice. The word "Dharma" is synoymous with Justice. That is why the Indian Judiciary has adopted the motto: "Yatho dharmasthatho jayah" meaning: "where there is Dharma, ther alone will be victory". This moto decorates the emblem of our Supreme Court. These words were borrowed from Mahabharata. They were uttered by Gandhari, the mother of the Kauravas. The context in which Gandhari uttered these mementous words conveys the more profound meaning of these words. Duryodhana before going to Mahabharata was comes to his mother Gandhari, falls at her feet and prays for her blessings for his success in the war. Gandhari was a great woman. Because her husband was blind, she voluntarily blindfolded herself life-long! This selfless tapasya endowed her with immense spiritual powers. Her words had tremendous powers. Whatever she uttered would always come true. If she had only uttered "Oh Son! You shall have victory", certainly Duryodhana would have won the battle! But though she knew that it was Duryodhana who was seeking her blessings, she deliberately told him:

"Yatho dharmas thatho jayah"

Duryodhana was not happy with these words. He thought his mother was oblivious of the fact that it was her own son who was seeking her blessings. He told his mother : "Oh! Maa! I am Duryodhana, your son who is seeking your blessings." She again told him : "Yatho dharmas thatho jayah". Duryodhana could not digest this answer. A bewildered Duryodhana told his mother slightly raising his voice : "Oh! Maa! I am Duryodhana, your son; your darling, seeking your blessings in the war for my success". Still, she again said :

"Yatho dharrnas thatho jayah"

Duryodhana could not get her blessings. Just see Gandhari's conduct. She did not bless her son deliberately. She loved him. He was her darling. But she knew that he was waging an unrighteous war. In her utter sense of impartiality with full dispassion, she only uttered these historical words :

"Yatho dharmas thatho jayah" in answer. These words mean more than mere : "Where Dharma is there is victory." They mean impartiality. They mean total dispassion. .They mean determination, They mean moral courage. That is why we have adopted these words as the motto of our Supreme Court.

Sri Narayan's book is very educative. I was really amazed to note that Naradasmriti had laid down as to the accountability of judges! It lays down that when 2 or more judges decide a case, they have to give only unanimous decision. What it means is when two or more judges sit to decide together, the decision should be of their collective mind. Individual mind may have-prejudice or it may swerve from the path of Dharma, but collective rriind will be more objective and more reasonable. This smriti further says that if the judges give any decision which may be opposed to the Srrrritis, or opposed to usage and convention or'which may be vitiated by friendship or hatred or greed or fear of the judges, then each judge has to be fined double of what the defeated party had to pay! There is another spiritual warning in Naradasmriti according to which, if an unjust decision is given, one fourth of the sin of injustice falls on the party who was adhaarmic to get this favourable unjust decision. The other 3/4th will fall (i) on the shoulders of witnesses who gave false deposition, (ii) on the shoulders of judges and (iii);on the shoulders of the king, equally.

I mentioned supra that Justice and Dharma are synonyms. Significantly it is mentioned in this marvelous work of Sri Narain that Kautilya called the courts as "Dharmashthiyas" and the judges as "Dharmasthas".

The author has given excerpts from original texts in Sanskrit and that way all ideas projected in his book are authentic and authoritative. The, book is very comprehensive and compact at the same time. The historical account of Judicial system in India from Vedic period upto pre-British period as traced in the Book"is interesting!

This book has to be kept and read in every library in India. It should be in the hands of every law-student. Mostly people think that we borrowed the British legal system and that ancient India has no idea of an established legal and judicial system. This book dispels this impression and makes every Indian proud of the ancient Glory of this country. The author Sir S. Narain deserves to be congraulated for his wonderful work.

(M.N. Krishnamani)
President,
Supreme Court Bar Association

REVIEW

The monograph of Sh. S. Narain on "Jail Judges and Justice in Ancient India" is a lucid expression of complicated subject. The author has beautifully crafted the whole manuscript into 11 chapters, each chapter reflects the depth of author about broad spectrum of law and justice. The language used by the author is so simple that every reader can enjoy the reading of such a manuscript. For any researcher in the area of criminal justice, the book can serve as a good resource.

I am impressed by the whole book in general and the chapter 6 & 7 in particular. The author has structured the hierarchy of courts in ancient India and the way the courts were handling the matter and disposing off them in speedy way. Reading of the whole book makes one to think that can we in India adopt such a system for the purpose of reducing the areas in courts, making justice speedy, transparent and affordable

Mr. S. Narain has written and published many books before it which have been appreciated by the eminent personalities in India. I find Mr. S. Narain a prolific writer, scholar, and a human being who cares for marginal sectors of society. The book can be useful for scholars, judges and students in the area of law and justice.

(S.C. Raina)
Prof. in-Charge

PREFACE

Hindu Law - the nucleus of Ancient Judicial system of India has been the oldest pedigree of any known system of jurisprudence as opined by many a scholars like John Myron.

The process of development of Hindu Law, called as Dharam-Vidya (science of sacred law) by Panini began with the composing of hymns of Vedas, which are regarded as the root as well as fountain head of all learnings including the sacred law blend with religious, moral and social values based upon the standard of conduct and the ancient philosophy of life. However, very little is known about the ancient system as to how the proceedings of court were conducted, how the witnesses were examined, how the defendant or accused was called upon and how the judgment was delivered. The methodology followed to extract truth from the accused and the ordeals conducted in cases where there was no eye witness and the modern kinds of narcotic tests and brain mapping technology were not available, is also unknown to common people.

At a time when the current judicial system is drawing flak from all quarters of society including eminent jurists and the judges at the highest echelon of judiciary, it is worthwhile to go into the ancient judicial system followed in different periods in ancient India. The book will perhaps provide a window to look through the ancient system and may be of interest to academicians of law and also the students of history who are keen to hae a deeper insight on the subject of law and justice.

(S. Narain)

MY SINCERE ACKNOWLEDGMENT

I am really grateful and indebted to Shri M.N. Krishnamani a noted jurist & senior advocate of supreme court of India for sparing valuable time to write this Keynote. The contents of his note speaks of his indepth knowledge of ancient scriptures and spiritual inclination. His causeless love for me left me spellound & impressed, which I can not forget.

I also express my sincere gratitude to Shri SNP Sinha, Chairman Bar Council of India for the **Forward Note** given by him for the book. His nice compliments about me show his affection for me from the core of his heart. Whenever I went to meet him he showered praise for the work even to his colleagues.

My sincere thanks to Dr. S.C. Raina, Professor & Head, Law Centre University of Delhi who has thoroughly read this book & reviewed it also. His comments and compliments about this book are source of inspiration & encouragement to me. Infact I do not deserve the praise he has showered calling me a learned person.

I am also thankful to Shri Vijay Kumar of Archological Society for providing excellent material for the book.

(S. Narain)

CONTENTS

1

Modern Justice and Ancient India

1

MODERN JUSTICE AND ANCIENT INDIA

"We find that people have started feeling that criminal trials are like (a) cobweb where small flies are getting caught and big people are dashing through" - ***Delhi Court***

A victim of justice under modern judicial system once goes to a court of law finds himself like a tiny boat in tempest, raised one moment on the foamy erest of a billow of hope and dashed down into a yawning chasm of despair the next, rolling at the mercy of witness, the lawyer he has hired and the judicial officer protracting the case for years and giving long dates of hearing and then to appeal and counter appeal to higher and still higher courts with no end in sight. According to a jurist the modern judicial system is a Jargon - a cobweb (spider's net) and once a person gets in, he would not get out easily.

The modern judicial system is a costly affair where in money plays a dominant role in hiring good lawyer, influencing the witness, roping in the lawyer of the opposite party and to appeal to higher echelon of court till he wins the case.

How a poor can approach the High Court or Supreme Court for redressal of injustice when the exorbitant fee of lawyer is much beyond his paying capacity.

According to a report compiled by the government 70% of the persons who got capital punishment i.e. death were those who would not have tons of money to fight the case to carry it on to the Supreme Court. This speaks itself the truth and is a sad commentary on the present Judicial system.

HOSTILE WITNESS

Witness or evidence in a case whether a civil or criminal are the back bone on which the entire case hinges and many a times the witnesses particularly in criminal cases retracts their earlier statement and turn hostile. This happens as abnormal period elapses between the filling of the case and deposing of witness and during this period all sort of pressures, threats are hurled on the witness to yield, to scumb to such mean tactics. Many a times the eyewitness in a case who stand adamant or firm are assaulted & murdered to get away with any evidence & defeat the case. There is no protection of witness from the side of govt. with the result that in many a

Criminal Justice System has Collapsed

- Supreme Court

Supreme Court sounded the grim warning that the criminal justice system had been subjugated with witnesses being manipulated and trials being hijacked and judges and lawyers remaining : "Handicapped witnesses"

TOI 12 Feb. 09

criminal cases of gruesome murder the culprits walk scot free in the absence of eyewitness, thus, eroding the faith on judiciary. Money also plays its part and the witnesses are offered heavy to heavier amount of money till they tempt and yield making a mockery of dispensation of justice.

NON-REGISTRATION OF CASES

In a criminal case the nearby police station is to be approached by a victim to file case against the accused. However it's an open secret that the police would avoid the registration of criminal case (FIR) with a view to show that the crime graph is not rising in the area covered by that police station. A common people has to request and request and approach the higher authorities and only there after the case is registered by the police. This is just to add salt to the injuries of a victim.

DELAY & DELAY, NO END - NO LIMIT

"Justice delayed is justice denied" the phrase perfectly applies to the modern system of dispensation of justice which is so cumbersome that years roll on even the decades pass and sometime victum dies but the final verdict in many cases not forthcoming. Since, the filling of the case in a metropolitan court, the first date or hearing comes after several months. Even the serving of summons/warrant are avoided congruently by the defendant. Thereafter framing the charges, witness, arguments & judgments in metropolitan court, all consume a period of several years. Appeal in district court then in high court, thereafter double judge Bench, there is no end of road. Sometimes the victim dies and leaves this world waiting & waiting for the justice which proves to be a wild goose chase.

The abnormal delay caused in concluding a case is mainly attributed to the fact that there is a long gap of time between the two consecutive dates of hearing say 2 to 6 months normally. As the disposal of the cases is not done expeditiously the new ones go on adding to the court with the result that arrears and backlog increase day by day and the courts are bogged down with workload. The total arrears of cases as reported in various news papers is as under :

From FIR to Judgement

- An FIR is registered at a local police station. Then it is sent to the area Metropolitan Magistrate's court within 24 hours.
- The police investigate the crime and file a chargesheet in the court. If the accused is in custody, the chargesheet has to be filed within 90 days; else the accused gets entitled to bail.
- The court takes note of the offence, issues warrants/summons for the accused to appear in court. The accused is given a copy of the documents. Cases like murder or rape, which attract punishment of over 7 years, are committed to a sessions court at this stage.
- The court starts argument before framing the final charges.
- The prosecution records the evidence. After that, the court examines and records the statement of the accused. Then the defence records the evidence.
- The court argues the case and then comes to the final arguments. The judge delivers the final judgement.

A murder or a rape case takes 4-7 years to be decided. Experts say the time taken has come down in the recent past. Senior criminal lawyer Ajay Dig Paul says the high-profile cases take longer because of constant media attention and appeals in higher courts at almost every stage.

BACKLOG OF CASES

Pendency :

2,52,55,982 Subordinate Courts

3,700,223 High Court

46,926 Supreme Court (Figure as on Sept. 30, 2007)

The position of National Capital Territory of Delhi is worst and in Delhi alone six lakh of the cases of various categories are pending, out of which around 2500 cases are of serious nature involving heinous crimes of grue some murder or so on.

Pending Cases for District Courts

Courts	Pending Cases
Additional Session Judge	18,012
Metropolitan Magistrate	6,14,851
Additional Distt. Judge	36,356
Civil Judge	65,282
Vehicle Accident Triennial	14,046
Rent Control Triennial	7,432
Industrial Triennial	948
Labour Court	14,183
Total	7,70,310

AREAR OF PENDING CASES OF COURTS

Session Court

Cases	Tis Hazari	Patiyala House	Karkardoma	Rohini	Total
Murder	242	391	264	505	1402
Etc.	1068	1900	1653	2274	6895
PCA	964	347	42	-	1353

Metropolitan Court

Cases	Tis Hazari	Patiyala House	Karkardoma	Rohini	Total
Police Challan	48512	57089	35674	63480	204755
NI Act-138 Complaint	70474	147097	101275	37548	356394
Cases	5796	7093	5349	5175	23413
Add. Act	3213	9805	7235	4109	24362
Subordinate Courts	900	1456	1395	1376	5127
Total					**614051**

(Source : Delhi Distt. Court website, 30 June 2007)

Question arises as to why the arrear of cases is allowed to increase at such as alarming rate. There are several reasons mainly the vacancies of Judges at the level of supreme court, high court, and even district court not being filled up promptly and several posts lie vacant for considerable period of time as under (till 30 June 2007) :

Judges	*Vacancy*
284	High Court
3233	Subordinate Courts

ACCOUNTABILITY OF JUDGES

Under the present system of dispensation of justice, judges enjoy considerable immunity and are almost not accountable for any lapse on their part, at the level of High court and Supreme Court. The process of impeachment for roping in a judge is very cumbersome. Signatures of minimum 100 MPs are necessitated to get off the ground, there is no institutionalized mechanism to investigate complaints against judges. Impeachment motions are impractical and hopelessly entangled in politics. To add to the worse a complaint against a judge is liable to be misconstrued as contempt of court inviting severe punishment and even imprisonment.

In the U.K., appointment of a judge can be challenged in the Judicial Appointments Commission, and the public also has a right to lodge a corruption or misconduct complaint against the judge to a Judicial Conduct Commissioner.

If a complainant was still not satisfied, an appeal could be made to the judicial ombudsman.

Asked to compare the transparency in judiciary's functioning with India, former CJI Justice Verma* said, "In United Kingdom, the conventions are still honoured, while in the

U.S., the law takes care of the safeguards. In India, the civil society has failed to put pressure for enforcement of accountability measures".

ANCIENT INDIA

On the contrary in ancient Indian system of dispensation of justice was simple, straight quick & almost free. Kauitlaya says that *"when in the court, the king shall never cause his petitioners to wait at the door"*.[1]

Just, imagine a glimpse of ancient system. The victim of injustice approaches the Darbar of the king or or the court of the town established by the king comprising of three learned judges[2], well versed in vedic text[4] dharmshatras well tested for integrity as well as honesty[3] and puts complaint in writing or oral about the wrong done to him. He gets a call on the same day or the next day for hearing. The defendant or accused is made to appear at the earliest, witnesses are called and the verdict is delivered. The witness or the defendent had to undergo certain ordeals to bring out the truth in absence of any witness or evidence, leaving not scope of turning the witness hostile or retracting its statement. There was hardly any role of money & the people had unstinted faith on judiciary.

Dharmasatras custom of the land, usages of local bodies ratiocination, and the opinion of the learned were the basic consideration for deciding a case. When all failed to solve the matter, the king was required to exercise his own diseretion in accordance with the Dharma.

ACCOUNTABILITY OF JUDGES IN ANCIENT INDIA

The ancient preceptors were aware of the human weakness and frequent failure of a person to adhere to the expected level of conduct and moral values and to be get tempted by the lust of wealth, sex, money or fame. The judges being the sons of the same soil were no exception, as such they were to face penal action in case of dereliction of their duties or to act with *extrenions* or *ulteriour* consideration or vested interest.

Nardasmriti says (lll.17)[5] that all the judges of the court should give a unanimous decision, and that then only the decision leaves no grievance (in the mind of the litigants). If the sabhayas give a decision,which is opposed to smriti and usage, through friendships, greed or fear each was liable to be fined twice as much as the fine to be paid by the defeated party (Nar.1.67)[6]. It was held that where an unjust decision is rendered, a quarter ofthe sin falls on the litigant (plaintiff or defendant) who is guilty of adharma, one quarter each on the witnesses, the sabhyas and the king.

Yajnavalkya Smriti also contains a similar provision in case a judge was found to act in voilation of the prescrbed norms of Dharma. There have been instances when the penal action was taken against Judges (Sabhyas) in case of any default on their part was proved.

REFRENCES

1. Kautilya 14.18.1

उपस्थानगतः कार्यार्थिनामद्वारासङ्गं कारयेत्। दुर्दर्शो हि राजा कार्याकार्यविपर्यासमासन्नैः कार्यते। तेन प्रकृतिकोपमरिवशं वा गच्छेत्। तस्माद्देवताश्रमपाषण्डश्रोत्रियपशुपुण्यस्थानानां बालवृद्धव्याधित -व्यसन्यनाथानां स्त्रीणां च क्रमेण कार्याणि पश्येत्; कार्यगौरवादात्ययिक वशेन वा।

2. Kautilya 56.57.1.1.

धर्मस्थास्त्रयस्त्रयोऽमात्या जनपदसन्धिसंग्रहणद्रोणमुखस्थानीयेषु व्यावहारिकानर्थान् कुर्युः।

तानां चामूढसंज्ञानामन्तरगारकृताः सिद्धयेयुः।

3. Kautilya - V. Gairola 1.1-2 pp. 26.

1) त्रिवगभयसशुद्धानमात्यान् स्वेषु कमेसु।
अधिकुर्याद् यथाशौचमित्याचार्या व्यवस्थिताः॥

2) न त्वेव कुर्यादात्मानं देवीं वा लक्ष्मी श्वरः।
शौचहेतोरमात्यानामेतत् कौटिल्यदर्शनम्॥

4. Yajna valkya II.2.

श्रुताध्ययनसंपन्ना धर्मशाः सत्यवादिनः।
राष्टा सभासदः कार्या रिपौ मित्रे च ये समाः॥2॥

किच, श्रुताध्ययनसंपन्नाः श्रुतेन मीमांसाव्याकरणादिश्रवणेन अध्ययनेन च देदाग्ययनेन संपन्नाः, धर्मज्ञाः, धर्मशास्ज्ञाः, सत्यवादिनः सत्यवचन-

5. Narda 3.17.

यत्र[4] सभ्यो जनः सर्वः साध्वेतदिति मन्यते।
स निःशल्यो विवादः स्यात् सशल्यः स्यादतोऽन्यथा॥17॥

6. Narda I. 67

[2]दुर्दृष्टे व्यवहारे तु सभ्यास्तं दण्डमाप्नुयुः।
न हि जातु विना दण्डं कश्चिन्मार्गोऽवतिष्ठते॥66॥
"रागादज्ञानतो वापि लोभाद्वा योऽन्यथा वदेत्।
सभ्योऽसभ्यः स विज्ञेयः तं पापं विनयेन्नृपः॥67॥

* H.T. & NBT News.

2

Ancient Concept of Law & Justice

2

ANCIENT CONCEPT OF LAW & JUSTICE

"A king who does his duty of protecting his people justly and according to law will go to heaven, whereas one who does not protect them or inflict punishment (to wrong doers) will not"

- Kautilya

God produced the transcendent body of law; since law is the king of kings, far more powerful and rigid, nothing can be mightier than law by whose aid, as by that of the highest monarch, even the weak may prevail over the strong." Thus the Hindus regard their laws – as part of religion *dharma* which rests entirely upon *Veda*, the word does not mean in that connection - the Vedic texts, but rather totality of knowledge, the sum of all understanding, of all religious and moral truths, whether revealed or not. It makes the universality of concept of dharma, i.e. morality. That is why the judges were

* Veda (Gloss of Sanca a). Sa Br. 14.4.2.23: Bri Ar Up 1.4.14.

named as Dharm Prabaktr or Dharmasthas means speaker of Dharma and fully rooted in Dharma. The courts were also accordingly termed as Dharmasthiya means place of Dharma.

Yajurveda[1] exhorts the king, the exponent of justice as follows (Ch. VI.1) :

"Just as I sanctify thee, the exponent of justice, for the display of knowledge, thee, the embodiment of truth, for spiritual advancement; the the administrator, for rule over the Earth; so should these justice loving people do."

"O king[2], thy first duty is to undertake the spread of knowledge and the administration of justice ...."

- Yajurveda VI.2

Another hymn prays as follows : "O noble king, like a father go near thy subject, and let the subjects like sons come near thee to seek protection. Just as fire is kindled with woodsticks, so hearthy complaint and kindle justice. Let versatile, learned and noble-minded queens, like mother, hear the complaints of women, and do justice unto them!"

"You magistrates who distinguish justice from injustice, listen to our grievances!"

"O[3] supreme king, endowed with knowledge, hear like sacrificing learned persons, our request made in an humble, laudatory tone!" (Y.V. VI. 26)

Yajurveda[4] also mentions the king as the master of all laws and the administration of justice as his duty. (Y.V. VII 36)

The aforesaid quotes from ancient scriptures make it clear that a king has been beholden as the exponent of justice and also the administrator of justice and enjoined with the duty of protection of society and individual through enforcement of standards of justice described in sacred literature i.e.'veda' Dharmasutras and Dharmashashtras etc.

Narada[6] (1.2) states 'when people were solely bent on dharma and were truthful, there existed neither administration of law and justice not hatred nor jealousy. When dharma declined among men, administration of law and justice came to be introduced and the king was declared to be the decider of disputes and the chastiser of the guilty'.

IMPARTIAL JUSTICE-WAY TO SALVATION

This is one of the master stokes of wisdom of ancients to link impartial administration of justice to the salvation of a king. As the king being the supreme authority of the State was likely to go astray and may act at his whim and fancy in the matter of delivery of justice. Linking of his salvation with the impartial justice will be a sufficient check to prevent him from acting in the arbitrary manner, violating the norms of Dharma and tenets of sacred law.

Yajnavalkya[8] says that "The Impartial administration of justice is a sacred duty of a king and yields to same reward as the solemn vedic sacrifice do."

"A king who does his duty of protecting his people justly and according to law will go to heaven, whereas one who does not protect them or inflict punishment to wrong doors will not" says Arthashashtra.[7]

The ancient preceptors were aware of the frequent failure of a man to act with proper conduct and moral values and therefore it remains the duty of the state to protect the society and individual by inflicting punishments on defaulters and use the coercive power abiding with principle of justice.

PRINCIPLE OF ANCIENT LAW & JUSTICE

"Law is blind" applies to modern law which doesn't discriminate between well enlightend and less enlightened, between moral & less-moral person, and between strong and weak person. The hammer of law strikes with the same intensity. However, if one stuff is strong and the other is weak, the same hammer-strike will make dents of different magnitude. The ancient system was designed in such a way that two different stuffs make equal dents in both the cases. Here the social strata was divided according to varna (Brahmin, Kshatriya, Vaishya and Sudra) feel the same effect of punishment for the same offence. If a Sudra pays a penalty of one rupee

MODERN LAW IS BLIND

Under modern judicial system, the hammer of law strikes with the same intensity turning a blind eye to the strength of stuff whether soft or hard with the result that the dent caused by the hammer will vary from stuff to stuff. This speakes the fallacy of modern system.

The Modern Goddess of Justice with Blind Eyes

the Khatriya will pay five or ten times more and so on. Manu one of the prominent law givers of Hindu society, while up holding the system mentions, similarly, *"When another common man would be fined one Kaarshaapana (copper or silver coin), the king shall be fined one thousand; that is the settled rule. In (a case of) theft the guilt of a sudra shall be eight fold that of a vaisya sixteenfold, that of a kshatriya two and thirty fold, that of the Brahmin sixty fourfold or quite a hundred fold, or (even) twice four and sixty fold, (each of them) know the nature of the offence".*

This means that, those who have more capability and are expected to know better should pay more and vice versa.

This above rationale is no doubt more logical and fair rather than applying the law blindly as the case under modern system.

A DEEPER INSIGHT INTO JURISPRUDENCE

The puranic scriptures of ancient India have endeavoured a new approach to the entire arena of jurisiprundance with a preventive and reformative wisdom. The 'Karma theory' says that any wrong act committed by you will recoil on you, in this life and the next life also. If you have killed a person wrongly or caused him damage making him suffer, you will meet the same fate in the next life. You will repay back in the same kind and none can save you'. This belief of Hindus prevents a person to commit any crime or wrong act.

A REFORMATIVE APPROACH

Dharma shastras of Hindus prescribe certain repentance/ purifying ordeals for many a crimes and wrong acts commited by a person like fasting for one to three days, undergoing penance performing certain yajnas etc. The idea is to make the person realize and repent for the crime or wrongful act commited by him intentionally or unintentionally and this brings out a total change and transformation without nurturing any ill-will or revengeful thoughts.

In view of the above, it will be seen that the conception of justice in ancient India was based upon high philosophy and deeper thoughts rather than inflicting usual sentence and punishment as the system prevailing in modern times.

FOOT NOTES

1. Y. Veda (VI.1)
   यवोऽसि यवयास्मद् द्वेषो यवयारातीर्दिवे -
   त्वाऽन्तरिक्षाय त्वा पृथिव्यै -
   त्वा झुन्धन्ताँल्लोकाः पितृषदनाः पितृषदनमसि॥
2. Y. Veda (VI.2)
   "द्यामग्रेणास्पृक्ष आन्तरिक्षं मध्येनाप्राः ...."
3. Y. Veda (VI.26)
   सोम राजन् विइवास्त्वं प्रजा उपावरोह -
   विइवास्त्व प्रजा उपावरोहन्तु।
   झृणोत्वग्निः समिधा हवं मे झष्टण्वन्त्वापो -
   धिषणाइच देवीः।

श्रोता ग्रावाणो विदुषो न यज्ञश्रृणोनु -
देवः सविता हवं मे स्वाहा॥

4. Y. Veda (VII.36)

उपयामगृहीतोऽसीन्द्राय त्वा मरुत्वत एष ते -
योनिरिन्द्राय त्वा मरुत्वते।
उपयामगृहीतोऽसि मरुतां त्वौजसे॥

5. Vajasheyi Samhita, XXX.10

''उत्सादेभ्यः कुब्जं प्रमुदे वामनं द्वाभ्यः स्राम
स्वप्नायान्धमधर्माय बधिरं पवित्राय भिषजं प्रज्ञानाय
नक्षत्रदर्शमाशिक्षायै प्रश्निनमुपशिक्षाया अभिप्रश्निनं
मर्यादायै प्रश्नविवाकम्॥

6. Narda 1.2.

[4]धर्मैकतानाः पुरुषा यदासन् सत्यवादिनः।
तदा न व्यवहारोऽभून्न द्वेषो नापि मत्सरः॥1॥
नष्टे धर्मे मनुष्याणां व्यवहारः प्रवर्त्तते।
द्रष्टा च व्यवहाराणां राजा दण्डधरः स्मृत॥2॥
[2]लिखितं राक्षिणश्चैव द्वौ विधी परिकीत्तितौ।
संदिग्धार्थविशुद्ध्यर्थः द्वयोर्विवदभानयोः॥3॥

7. Kautilya

4) स्वधर्मः स्वर्गायानन्त्याय च। तस्यातिक्रमे लोकः सङ्करादुच्छिद्येत।
5) तस्मात्स्वधर्मं भूतानां राजा न व्यभिचारयेत्।
स्वधर्मं संदधानो हि प्रेत्य चेह च नन्दति॥

8. Yaj- 1. 39.

यो दण्डयान्दण्डयेद्राजा सम्यग्वध्यांश्च घातयेत्।
इष्टं स्यात्क्रतुभिस्तेन समाप्तवरदक्षिणैः॥359॥

3

Sources & Autorities of Hindu Law

3

SOURCES & AUTORITIES OF HINDU LAW

"Hindu Law has the oldest pedigree of any known system of jurisprudence, and even now it shows no signs of decrepitude".

- John Myron.

Believed to be the revealed words of God, Hindus regard the Vedas as the fountain head of all learnings including the sacred law blend with religious, moral and social values embracing dharma based upon the standard of conduct and philosophy of life. With the passage of time, the learning of Vedas became more and more obscure and beyond the comprehension of common people and there was a need to outline the religious, moral, social and legal duties for guidance of society. As such sutra literatre comprising of smritis Grahsutras, Dharmasutras came up containing the regulations on all such matters in simple and precise manner. The *Smrtis* embody the law proper, both substantive and adjective. The *Sutras* were devised for the study of the *Vedas;* those, which related to law and practical life, were called the *Dharma Sutras.* Another group of texts called *Dharmasastra* may be divided into three, viz., the *Smritis* including *Samhitas,* the *Vyakhyana* or Glosses and Conmmentaries upon the *Smritis,* and finally *Nibandhana Grantha* or *Digests.* All these texts are the sources of ancient Indian laws and judicial system.

SMRITIS – GIVERS OF HINDU LAW

Out of ancient massive literature, containing scattered reference on legal matters, Smrities are regarded as the main and direct source of Hindu law. Manu Smriti; Narda smirti and Yajanavalka smrities are more specific in this regard.

MANUSMRITI

Manusmriti also called Dharmashastra is regarded as the most authorative on Hindu law. The age of Manu and also Manusmriti is shrouded into antiquity. The Manusmriti has been getting additions from time to time at a much later date and the contents were compiled into a compendium known as **Manusmriti.**

Who was Manu? What was his age and birth? is again mired into uncertainty.

In the Rgveda the rsis often speak of Manu as 'father' (Rg. I.80.16, I.114.2, VIII.63.1) without explicitly saying 'of whom'. But in Rg. II.33, 13 the sage speaks of Manu as 'out father'. The word Manu in several cases and in compound words like 'Manu-jata', 'Manu-pritasah' and 'Manu-hita' occur hundreds of times. In many of the verses of the Rg. in which the word Manu occurs, commentators and translators often hold that the word Manu stands for 'Manusya' (and not merely for Manu as an individual). But it is clear that in some Rgveda verses Manu has been taken as an individual sage; eg. In Rg. I.II2.16 a prayer is made to the Asvins to come with help as they did in the past ages in the case of Sayu, Atri and Manu.

However, the *Chhandogya* upnishada and even in *Nirukta*, Manu has definite been mentioned as a 'law giver' and a legal authority. The various Dharmasutras also mention Manu as a pioneer legal authority.

CONTENTS

Manu Smriti containing 2,694 stanzas in 12 chapters deals with cosmogony, Dharma, the sacraments, initiation and Vedic study, forms of marriage, hospitality and funerary rites, dietary laws, pollution and purification, rules for women and wives, royal law, many sorts of juridical matters, and also more religious matters, which include donations, rites, the doctrine of karma, the soul, and punishment in many sort of hells.

As regards the law and justice, Manusmriti describes the king as the supreme authority of the state who is supposed to establish authority and protect the people with Danda, a symbol of power which, if he does not inflict punishment on those worthy to be punished, the stronger would roast the weaker like a fish on a spit. According to Manu the punishment inflicted to the criminals would vary keeping in the view the strength and weakness of a person. Manu says, *"When another common man would be fined one kaarshaapana (copper or silver coin), the king shall be fined one thousand; that is the settled rule"*. In (a case of) theft, the guilt of a '*sudra* shall be eight fold, that of a *vaishya* sixteen fold, that of a Kshatriya two-and- thirtyfold, that of a Braahman. Sixty four fold, or quite a hundredfold, or (even) twrice four-and sixty fold, (each of them) knowing the nature of the offence.

This means those who have more capability and are expected to know better should pay more and vice-versa.

One of the chief duties of the king is the maintenance and protection of the *'Varna'* system through his power of da-n-da. This is so and the king is obeyd because it is realized that varna and the State are necessary aids to the achievement of the final goal of life.

The sources of Dharma are stated by Manu to be (a) *Veda* or *Sruti,* (b) *Smriti* or *Dharma-sastra,* (c) *Sila,* and (d) *Acharo,* the customs of holy men. Doubtful points of Dharma were to be settled by a body of experts, of *Sishtas,* (well-versed in sacred law), which was called Parishad.

Manu smriti also provides guidance to a king to deal with legal cases which are divided into eighteen heads[7] and also mentions the procedure of witness and ordeals.

YAJNAVALKYA SMRITI

The name of Yajnavalkya is one of the most illustrious among the Vedic sages. He is credited with having promulgated the White Yajurveda. In the Brhadaranya Upanishad Yajnavalkya appears as a great philosopher teaching the recondite doctrines of Brahma and immortality to one of his two wives, the philosophically minded Maitreyi (Brhad. Up. II.4 and IV.5). Yajnavalkya is also said to have imparted to Janaka the knowledge of the destiny of the soul after it is released from the bonds of flesh and wordly affections.

Yajnavalkya's work is more systematic than that of Manu. He divides the work into three sections and relegates all topics to their proper positions and avoids repetition. He treats almost all subjects that we find in Manu.

As far as judicial administration is concerned Kanda II of the smriti mentions members of the hall of justice, judge, definition of vyavaharapada, rules of procedure, plaint, reply, taking security and kinds of litigation cases.

Besides the four Vedas, Yajnavalkya refers to the Vedangas as six and enumerates fourteen vidyas (four Vedas, six angas, purana, nyaya, mimamsa, dharmasastra). He refers to the Aranyaka and Yogasastra composed by himself. He enumerates at the commencement, nineteen authors on dharma, besides himself. He lays down the dictum that where dharmasastra and arthasastra conflict, the former shall prevail (Yajnavalkyasmriti II. 21).

Administeration of Justice

Yajnavalkyasmriti (1.327) says that the administration of justice was the personal concern of the king. The Mitakshara on Yajnavalkya II. 1 states that protecting the subjects is the highest duty of a king and that that duty cannot be discharged without eradication and punishing the wikcked, which latter requires that the king should administer justice (vyavaharadarsana).

Yaj. (I. 359-360) declares that the impartial administration of justice yields the same rewards as solemn Vedic sacrifices do. In this way administration of justice was held to be a very sacred duty.

Yaj (II.8 and 305) appears to distinguish between vivada (law-suit) and vyavahara (judicial procedure). Yaj. (II.5) defines "If a person, who is set at naught by others in a manner that is opposed to the rules of smriti and to good usage or conventions, informs the king (or his judge), that is a 'Vyavaharapada'.

Titles of Legal Cases

Yajnavalkya mentions the following titles of vyavaharapada. They are rnadana, upanidhi, asvamivikraya, sambhuya-samuthana, dattapradanika, vetanadana, samvid-vyatikrama, kritanusaya, vikriyasampradana, svamipalavivada, simavivada, vakparushya, dandaparushya, steya, sahasa, strisangrahana, dayavibhaga, dyutasamahvaya, abhyupteyasusrusha, prakirnaka, etc.

Yaj. 11.23 speaks of arthavivada (civil dispute) and so makes a distinction between civil and criminal disputes.

According to Yaj. II.8 vyavahara is chatushpad- having four feet, viz., plaint, the reply, the proof (kriya) and decision (nirnaya).

Dispensing of Justice

Justice was to be primarily dispensed by the king. Yaj. II. provides that the king wearing no gaudy dress or ornaments is to enter the sabha (the hall of justice) for looking into the causes of litigants, accompanied by learned brahnianas and ministers proficient in statecraft, is to be free from hot temper and greed and decide according to the law laid down in dharmasastras. Mitakshara on Yajnavalkyasmriti (II.2) says that a king who examinies disputes in the presence of the judge, the ministers, learned brahmanas, the purohita and the sabhyas attains heaven. As regards points of law the king or judge is required to decide according to the rules of dharmasastra (Yaj. II. 1).

If the king cannot attend to the work of administering justice because of some other duties, the king should appoint a learned brahmana together with three sabhyas to decide the disputes of people (Yaj. II. 3). The chief judge was preferably to be a learned brahmana (Yaj. II.3) and the king should appoint at least three sabhyas to associate with the Chief Judge in the disposal of suits. Yaj. II.2 also requires the qualifications of the sabhyas which are similar to those of the Naradasmriti (III. 4-5).

Judges not immune to Penal Action

If the sabhyas give a decision, which is opposed to smriti and usage, through friendship, greed or fear, each was liable to be fined twice as much as the fine to be paid by the defeated party (Yaj. II.4).

Yaj. 1.30 states that law-suits may be dicided by village councils (kulani), corporations (sreni), assemblies (puga), the judges appointed by the king and the king himself. Howevere, Yajnavalkya refers to only two State Courts, viz., that of the chief justice and that of the king himself.

Yaj. II. 6 prescribes when the defendant comes before the court, the information at first given by the plaintiff is to be written down accurately in his presence together with the year, month, fortnight, day, names (of parties), caste, etc.

Witness & Ordeals

Yajnavalkyasmriti also speaks of means of proof such as documents, witnesses, ordeals, etc. However, ordeals are to be resorted to only when the human means are not available (Yaj. II. 22).

The last stage in a judicial proceeding is siddhi (Yaj. II.8) or nirnaya (decision). A jayapatra (a document of success ie. Judgment) should be given to the successful party in befitting manner after signing on it.

Yajnavalkya's holistic approach on jurisprudence enabled him to occupy one of the prominent positions among the legal authorities such as Manu and Narada.

NARADASMRITI

Narada is not mentioned by Yajnavalkya in the list of ancient writers on dharma, nor does Parasara mention him. Visvarupa, however, quotes a verse of Vrddha-Yajnavalkya, where Narada is the first among ten expounders of dharma enumerated therein. Narada is a very ancient name. The Manusmriti (1.35) mentions Narada as one of the ten primeval Prajapatis. In the Mahabharata sage Narada figures frequently. Santi Parva (30.6) says that Narada was the maternal uncle of Parvata.

Narada (1.2) says that the administration of justice was the personal concern of the king. Narada (1.2) states ' when[1] people were solely bent on dharma and were truthful, there existed neither administration of law and justice not hatred nor jealousy. When dharma declined among men, administration of law and justice came to be introduced and the king was declared to be the decider of disputes and the chastiser of the guilty.[1]

Narada (I. 1) mentions the word vyavahara 'a dispute or a law-suit.The Naradasmriti contains three chapters on the

principles of judicial procedure (vyavahara-matrka) and on the judicial assembly (sabha) and deals with 18.

It will be noticed that Narada follows the Manusmriti to a considerable extent in the nomenclature and the arrangement of the eighteen titles. Narada (I. 16-19) has the same 15 topics as those of Manu (some of the titles are differently named by Narada, eg. he speaks of upaniḍhi, while Manu employs the word nikshepa), omits svamipalavivada, steya and strisangrahana, adds abhyupetyasusrusha and another topic viz prakirnaka and splits krayavikrayanusaya into two, viz., kritanusaya and vikriyasampradana. He includes steya under sahasa and also in what is an appendix.

Guilts & Crimes

Narada relegates all matters in which the king would take action suo motu to a separate topic, prakirnaka, about which he says 'under prakirnaka are comprised lawsuits depending on'the king (i.e. on the king's own action) such as transgressions of the king's commandments and obedience to his injuctions, grants of towns, dissensions among the constituent elements (such as ministers) of the State, the duties and breaches thereof among heretics, followers of the Veda, corporations (of merchants) and groups, dispute between father and son, neglect of prescribed penances, abstraction of gifts made to worthy persons, the wrath of hermits, sinful confusion of castes and the rules regarding their maintenance and,in short, whatever matter has been omitted in the preceding (vyavaharapadas) - these are treated under prakirnaka'[2].

The ten aparadhas according to Narada are: disobedience of the king's order, murder of a woman, confusion of varnas, adultery , theft, pregnancy from one not the husband, abuse and defamation, abscenity, assault (dandaparushya), abortion. They were called aparadhas because they were met with fine. It will be noticed that some of these come under several vyavaharapadas and some like varnasankara are included in prakirnaka by Narada (V.4).

Qualification of Judges

Narada also describes the qualifications of a judge. He requires: The judge should be proficient in the texts on the eithteen titles of law, their 8000 sub-heads, in logic (anvikshiki) and should be master of the Veda and Smritis. Just as a physician takes out from the body an iron dart by the employment of surgical instruments, so a judge should extricated from a law-suit the deceit (underlying it)'[3].

A judge was generally styled pradvivaka. It occurs in Narada (I. 35). The word is a combination of prad (one who puts questions to the suitors, from the root pracch) and vivaka (who speaks out or analyses the truth, from the root vac with vi). Such derivation is given by Narada.

Narada (III.4) states that the king should appoint sabhyas (or members of the court of justice) to associate with the Chief Judge in the disposal of suits. Narada (III 4-5) requires the following qualification in the sabhyas: they should be endowed with the study of the Vedas, should know dharmasastra, should speak the truth, should be impartial to friend or foe, should be steady, devoted to their work, intelligent, hereditary, proficient in arthasastra. Impartiality in the king and the judges is insisted ,on in the text(Narada I. 34, III. 5).

Judging & Judgement

Narada III. 17 requires that all the judges of the court should give a unanimous decision, and that then only the decision leaves no grievance (in the mind of the litigants).[5] If the sabhyas give a decision, which is opposed to smriti and usage, through friendship, greed or fear, each was liable to be fined twice as much as the fine to be paid by the defeated party (Nar. 1.67). It was held that where an unjust decision is rendered a quarter of the sin falls on the litigant (plaintiff or defendant) who is guilty of adharma, one quarter each on the witnesses, the sabhyas and the king.

The chief justice, the sabhyas and the learned brahmanas were probably elderly people, as great emphasis-is laid on this by Narada(III.18).

Besides the king's court of justice there were other tribunals also (Nar. I.7).[6] It states that law-suits may be decided by village councils (kulani), corporations (sreni), assemblies (gana), the judges appointed by the king and the king himself, each later one being superior to each preceding one.

Summoning of Accused / Defendent

Very elaborate rule are laid down about the summoning of the defendant or accused by Narada (I. 52-54). Narada prescribes that cowherds when it is the season for taking cows for grazing, agriculturists in the sowing season, artisans actually engaged in work and soldiers engaged in war should not be summoned to appear in person, while so engaged. In these cases some one on their behalf should be summoned as a representative. But it is provided that even these persons may be summoned with proper safeguards in important cases or grave charges, such as the killing of human beings, theft, rape, eating forbidden food, counterfeiting coins, high treason, etc.

In the case of those who are exempted from personal appearance their relatives or some other person appointed by them or one who can be recognized as their agent may be allowed to appear. However, according to Narada, if a person who is not a brother nor father nor son nor appointed to represent another prosecutes a law-suit for another, he is liable to be fined.

The plaintiff may put under restraint till the approach of the bailiff by the king's order the defendant. A defendant would not be liable to be fined, if he disregards a restraint order which ties him down to a river ford, or to a forest, to a bad place (infested by thieves and tigers) or at the time of an invasion (Narada I. 49).

Evidence & Witness

Narada IV 145 says that no oral evidence should be allowed to contradict the terms of a document, that the mode of proving a matter by a document is always superior.

Several verses of Narada lay down the contents of the judgment. It was to contain a brief statement of the plaint, the reply, the evidence, the depositions of witnesses, discussion thereof, arguments, the Smriti texts applicable, the opinion of the sabhyas, the decision and the relief granted, and should be signed by the chief justice and bear the royal seal. Even present judicial system follows the same method of judgment.

THE WORKS OF MADHAVACHARYA

Madhavacharya is the brightest star in the galaxy of dakshinatya authors on dharmasastra. He along with Vidyaranya caused the founding of the city of Vijayanagara. Among the works of Madhavacharya, two deserve special mention, viz., the Parasara- madhaviya his commentary on the Parasarasmriti and the Kaalanirnaya, the others being Kaalamadhava, Jivanmuktiviveka, panchadasi, Jaiminiya-nyayamalavistara, vaiyasika- nyayamalavistara, etc.

Vachaspatimisra was the foremost nibandha writer on Smriti in Mithila. His Vivadachintamani had been recognized by the High Courts in India and by the Judicial Committee of the Privy Council as a work of paramount authority on matters of Hindu Law in Mithila. His literary activity was closely connected with the reigns of two kings of Mithila, viz. Bhairavendra or Bhairavasimha (also called Harinarayana) and his son Ramabhdra (called also Rnnanaravana both of the Kamesvara dvnasty. Vachasnatimisra has written many works like Acharachintamani, Ahnikachintamani, Suddhichintamani, Dvaitachintamani, Krityachintamani, Nityachintamani, Vyavaharachintamani, Vivadachintamani, etc, etc.

His Vivadachintamani deals exhaustively with the eighteen titles of law (vyvaharapadas). The Vyvaharachintamani deals with judicial procedure, viz., the four principal topics thereof, viz. bhasha (the plaint), uttara (reply of defendant), kriya (evidence), nirnaya (decision).

KAUTILYA'S ARTHASHASTRA

Chanakya (Kautilya) was the minister and monitor of Chandragupta Maurya - a famous historical figure having overthrown the mighty empire of Nanda kings under the guidance of Chanakya and became the first monarch of Maurya Dynasty who ruled India for centuries with empire overflonking to a part of Afghanistan.

Kautilya regarded as the first management guru, his thoughts and ideas helped the kings to rule for centuries. Kautilya's Arthashastra is a work of Mauryan Period and covers a wide range of topics like statecraft, politics, military warfare, strategy, selcion and training of employees, leadership skills, legal systems, accounting systems, taxation, fiscal policies, civil rules, and technicl subjects like medicine, gemology, metallurgy, measures of length, tables of weights etc. The book also contains chapters on civic rules and judicial administration and was beholden with respect and guidance by the Mauryan kings. All the powerful kings in ancient India like Ashoka had learnt Arthashastra and practiced it to expand their kingdom multifold to protect the kingdom against powerful enemies, and develop winning strategies, habits and practices.

MITAKSARA

The Mitaksara a work of 11th century is a legal commentary on the Yajnavalkya Smriti by vijanesvara, who lived near the end of the eleventh century during the reign of Vikramaditya VI of the Chalukya dynasty and was a scholar in western Chalukya court and perhaps was Judge as opined by kane.

The work provides commentary with outside opinions about the same passages of the text of earlier commentators as well, including medhatithi etc. The most important topics include property rights, property distribution, and inheritance. The text has become the authority, especially on inheritance, throughout most of India even after independence.

Ancient India has produced many prominent writers on Dharmasastra during a period of several centuries. All these authors and their works were actuated by the most laudable motives of regulating the Aryan society in all matters civil, religious and moral, and of securing happiness in this world and the next. They laid greatest emphasis on the duties of every man as a member of the whole Aryan society, as a member of the particular class to which he belonged and very little emphasis on the privileges of men.

FOOT NOTES

1. धर्मैकतानाः पुरूषा यदासन्सत्यवादिनः।
   तदा न व्यवहारोऽमून्न द्वेषो नापि मत्सरः॥
   नष्टे धर्मे मनुष्याणां व्यवहारः प्रवर्तते।
   द्रष्टा च व्यवहाराणां राजा दण्डधरः स्मृतः॥

   - Narda I.2

2. प्रकीर्णके पुनर्ज्ञयो व्यवहारो नृपाझयः।
   राज्ञामाज्ञाप्रतीघातस्तत्कर्मकरणं तथा॥
   पुरप्रदानं संभेदः प्रकृतीनां तथैव च।
   पाखण्डिनैगमश्रेणीगण धर्मविपर्ययः॥
   पितापुत्रविवादश्च प्रायश्चितव्यक्रिमः॥
   प्रतिग्रहविलोपश्च कोपश्चाश्रमिणामपि॥
   वर्णसङ्करदोषश्च तद्रवृत्तिनिधमस्नथा।
   न दृष्टं यश्च पूर्वेषु सर्व तत्स्यात्प्रकीर्णकम्॥

   Narda (प्रकीर्णक 1-4) quoted by the Mitakshara on Yajnavalkya II. 295

3. अष्टादड्ापदामिज्ञस्तद्मदाष्टसहस्रवित्।
   आन्वीक्षिक्यादिकुड्ालः श्रुतिस्मृतिपरायणः॥
   यथा ड्ाल्यं मिषक्कायादुद्दरेद्यन्त्रयुक्तिभिः।
   प्राड्विवाकस्तथा ड्ाल्यमुद्धरेदव्यवहारतः॥

   Narda quoted in स्मृतिचन्द्रिका II

4. राजा तु धार्मिकान् सभ्यान्नियुञ्ज्यात् सुपरीक्षितान्।
व्यवहारघुरं वोढुं ये शक्ताः सद्गवा इव॥4॥
धर्मशास्त्रार्थकुशलाः कुलीनाः सत्यवादिनाः।
समा शत्रौ च मित्रे नृपतेः स्युः सभासदः॥5॥
तत्प्रतिष्ठः स्मृतो धर्मा धर्ममूलश्च पार्थिवः।

Narada III.2

5. यत्र स्भ्यो जनः सवः साध्वेतदिति मन्थते।
स निःङाल्यो विवादः स्यात् सङाल्यः एयादतोन्यथा॥

Narada III.17

6. कुलानि श्रेणयश्चैव गणश्चाधिकृतो नृपः
प्रतिष्ठा व्यवहाराणां गुर्वेभ्यस्तुत्तरोत्तरम्॥

Narada I.7

7. तत्रासीनः स्थितो वापि पाणिमुद्यम्य दक्षिणम्।
विनीतवेषाभरणः पश्येत्कार्याणि कार्यिणाम्॥2॥
प्रत्यहं देहशद्दष्टैश्रव शासछ्ष्टैश्रव हेतुभिः।
अष्टादशसु मार्गेषु निबद्धानि पृथक्पृथक्॥3॥
तेपामाद्यमृणादानं निक्षेपोऽखामिविक्रयः।
संभूय च समुत्थानं दत्तस्यानपकर्म च॥4॥
वेतनस्यैव चादानं संविद्श्रव व्यक्क्रिमः।
क्रयविक्रयानुशयो विवादः स्वामिपालयोः॥5॥
सीमाविवादधर्मश्रव परारूण्ये दण्डवाचिके।
स्तेयं च साहसं चैव स्त्रीसंग्रहणमेव च॥6॥
स्त्रींपुंधर्मो विभागश्रव द्यूतमाह्वय एव च।
पदान्यष्टादशैतानि व्यवहारस्थिताविह॥7॥

Manu 3.2-7

4

Judicial System of Ancient India

4

JUDICIAL SYSTEM OF ANCIENT INDIA

The impartial administriation of justice yields the same rewards as solemn vedic sacrifices do.

- Yajnavalkya 1.359

Ancient India has seen several phases with consistent growth, development and advancement keeping with the change in political set up & socio-economic conditions of that period : The judicial system did also undergo simultaneous updating and refinement to respond the call of the time, to maintain peaceful social order and to protect the weaker from the wicked and powerful.

VEDIC PERIOD

Vedic period is regarded as the dawn & meridian of Aryan civilization which was fairly developed. The Vedas provide a glimpse of a society which was rather liberal, compassionate, caring and the women were allowed to take part in all religious rites like yajnas and many of them have made spiritual lineage. The society was not fragmented by the rigid caste system as transpires from a hymn of Rig Veda quoted as under :

"We the different men have different aptitudes & pursuits. The carpenter deals with broken things, the physician a patient, the priest some one who will perform sacrifice".

POLITICAL & JUDICIAL SET UP

The political setup consisted of small kingdoms, each ruled by a king appointed through election or on *hereditary* basis. The king was assisted by Kul Prohita & senani or minister in day to day judicial as well as political matters. The witness would also be subjected to religious ordeals to extract truth.

The Judicial set up was, decentralized in the sense that serious cases were entertained in the royal court while the common ones of civil as well criminal nature were decided by village sabha & *smiti*, both were powerful bodies enjoined with *administration* as well as judicial functions.

The village sabha was headed by Gram vadini. The executive body of Sabha consisting of the representatives of groups of families which would meet and handover the case to a panel of three members of the executive body, well versed in legal matters. The village sabha was autonomous in its functioning. Great prominene is given in the *RigVeda* on two state level assemblies called *sabha* and *samiti* which seem to have formed an essetial feature of the government. We possess no definite information about the composition of the either, or the distinction between the two. Most probably the *samiti* at state level mainly dealt with policy decisions and political business and judicial matter included common people while the the *sabha*, less political in character, was a more select body of the Elders or Nobles.

It was through these two assemblies that the will of the people on important matters of the *rashtra* was expressed. There is ample evidence in Athrav Veda to suggest that smiti acted as court of law also.

LATER VEDIC PERIOD
(1000 B.C. – 600 B.C.)

This period witnessed further advancement in material civilization. Various positive sciences and technology grew and developed to a new height. Aryans made advancement to upper Gangetic plains i.e. Eastern U.P., Bihar etc. and set up their kingdoms each ruled by a king. An intensive lust to add more & more territory to their kingdom is particularly noticed among them even at the cost of of waging war against the weaker kingdom. The famous Mahabharta war between Kaurva & Pandva was fought during the period over the territory issue, settled through forced battle.

WORKING OF COURTS AND PROCEEDINGS

Working of a court in later vedic period was simple, plain & fully transparent. The victim would go to the royal Darbar or the court of judges established by the king and would lodge complaint to a designated functionary of clerical level in writing or verbally who would pass on the same to the king through the minister. The victim would be called upon to present his case and the accused will be summoned, witness and evidence will also be examined at the sametime. The accused could be asked to prove his innocence through a religious ordeal if no witness is available and the verdict would be given immediately. No cumbersome formalities of affedevit was adjoined. No further dating for hearing as in the present system framing of charges etc and No fee for lawyers. The judgement was quick and with out any expenditure on the part of accused or the victim.

In case of village court where village 'sabha' was the competent body for disposal of the cases, the Head of Sabha would settle the minor disputes. However for others the meeting of executive body was generally convened.

JUDICIAL SYSTEM

The administrative and Judicial system, except some minor changes, continued as in Vedic period. However kings of respective kingdom asserted authority more & more and became powerful. Attrey Brahmna, a work of contemporary period mentions five kinds of administrative cum judicial setup with king as the supreme authority. The judicial system in vedic as well as later vedic period was found on Dharma and the society as well as king both were bound by Dharma. The rural courts were of three kinds :

(i) Kula

(ii) Shreni and

(iii) Gana

Kula - an association of families & kins-man, and Shreni was the association of person of different castes but practising the same craft. Gana was a federation of all these associations and comprised the whole village republic[1]. The Kula, Shreni and Gana functioned as courts of law- subordinate to the kings court and to the king himself as final court of appeal.

However, the judges there in, had the approval from the king who was also empowered to make any changes there in and also to constitute special court for prompt justice to the people. The study of contemporary literature shows that many a times spies were deployed to investigate the case and to report the facts to the king. Special care was exercised to ensure that an innocent person does not get punishment and a serious view was taken in case the higher court lets of the accused person and the judge of the trial court was subjected to intensive serutiny to see if any favouritism or leniency was shown to the either party.

AGE OF NANDA AND MAURYAS (600 BC – 100 BC)

This period witnessed a major political shake up when a strong empire of Magdha ruled by Nanda kings with its capital at Patliputra was overthrown by Chandra Gupt Maurya who took the reign of the state with his menter Chankya as the minister to advice and guide him in all important matters. This period is also marked by a galaxy of preceptors who framed the regulations and religious rituals for day to day life including the dispensation of law and justice. Their works titled as Smrities and Dharm sutra most notable being Manu Smriti, Yajna Valka smriti, Narada Smriti, are considered as the legal authority for Hindu law. Criminal and civil cases were tried in separate courts. However a notable feature was that the laws and punishments were not uniform for all castes as the four varna system firmly gripped the society in those days. Crimes commited against the Brahmanas and higher castes people were severely treated while crimes against shudras were taken leniently.

LEGAL AND JUDICIAL SYSTEM

By and large and Judicial system was influenced by the regulations given in smrities and dharm sutras. Arithshastra of Kautilya written by Chanakya is the most important work from law and Judicial point of view. It is the Dharam sutras and smrities that we find the real beginning of civil and criminal law.

LAW AND SMRITIES

Ancient smritis divide the lawsuits and judicial proceedings *(vyavaharpadas)* into two categories civil and criminal. They more or less deal with most of the subjects brought out in modern manner. They also divide laws into substantive and adjective or procedural manner. The vyavaharapadas correspond to the former and the rules about procedure, the appointment of judges and the constitution of courts, evidence and limitations are adjective law.

ADJECTIVE LAW

The smrtis lay down a high level of judicial procedure, but the procedure must have been modified to suit the requirements of different times and the resources and inclinations of different kings.

Justice was to be primarily dispensed by the king. He was an original court as well as an appellate tribunal. *Smrtis* and digests insist that the king cannot dispense justice by himself alone, but must do so with the help and guidance of other, learned persons Manu[2] and Yajnavalkya[3] provide that the king wearing no gaudy dress or ornaments is to enter the *sabha* (the Hall of Justice) for looking into the cases of litigants, accompanied by learned *Brahmanas* and minister proficient in statecraft, is to be free from hot temper and greed and decide according to the law laid down by *Dharmasastras.*

TYPE OF COURTS

According to Brhaspati, a Court of Justice was of four kinds:

1. **pratishthita,** one established in a fixed place such as a town
2. **apratishtita,** not fixed in one place, but moving from place to place as on a circuit
3. **mudrita,** the court of a judge appointed by the king, who is authorized to use the royal seal, and
4. **sasita,** i.e., the court in which the king himself presides

The *Sabha* is said to have ten *angas* by Brhaspati, they are :

1. The King
2. The Chief Judge appointed by the king
3. The Sabhyas

4. Smrti
5. Ganaka (accountant)
6. Lekhala (the scribe)
7. Gold
8. Fire
9. Water
10. Svapurusha / Sadhyapala (bailiff)

The chief judge declares the law, the king awards punishment, the *Sabhyas* examine the dispute, *Smritis* lay down the rules of decision, the success (of one party or the other) and the punishment; gold and fire are required for taking oaths, the water is for men when they feel thirsty, the *Ganaka* counts subject matter of dispute, the scribe writes down the pleadings, depositions and the decision, the *Purusha* summons the *Sabhyas*, the defendant, the witnesses, and the guards, the complainant and the defendant when they have furnished no surety.

LAWYERS

So far as the smritis are concerned there is nothing to show that any class of persons whose profession was the same as that of modern counsels, solicitors, or legal practitioners and those who were regulated by the State, existed. In the commentary of *Asahaya* as edited by Kalyanabhatta or Narada, there is an instructive story from which it appears that persons who had studied the *smrtis,* helped parties in return for monetary considerations to raise contentions before the court. According *Sukranitisara*[4] the person who is appointed to represent a party should get as his wages 1/6, 1/20, 1/40, 1/80 or 1/160 part of the amount in dispute, that the wages become less and less as the claim in dispute becomes higher or if several persons employ one representative. One who knows *dharmasastra* and the procedure of lawsuits should be appointed as representative and not any one who is deficient in these; if the representative takes wages without knowing these he should be punished by the king. A representative is to be appointed by the party and not by the king at his will, if the representative allows the matter entrusted to him to fail owing to his greed he is liable to be fined. In the *Questions of Milinda*[5] one passage mentions *dhammasetthino* (bankers of dharma), which word reminds us of the *sresthin* in the *Mrcchakatika*. The *dhammapanikas* probably correspond to lawyers. (The word *vakeel* means agent).

COURT FEES

In disputes of a criminal nature no court fees had to be paid in ancient India. As regards civil disputes also nothing had to be paid at the inception of the suit. However certain rules are prescribed by the *Arthasastra*,[6] *the Yajnavalkyasmrti, the Naradasmrti, the Vishnudharmasutra* and others about payments to the king after the suit is decided. The guilty was certainly fined by the king.

JUDICIAL SYSTEM OF MAURYAN RULERS

"A king who does his duty of protecting his people justly and according to law will go to heaven, whereas one who does not protect them or inflicts unjust punishment will not" SAYS Arthasastra[5]. Mauryan legal system covers civil law and criminal law. The judge was called a *dharmastha* – upholder of *dharma. Pradeshtr* (magistrates) were another class of judicial officers.

Both judges and magistrates were subordinates of the *Samahatr,* the Chancellor. There were benches of three judges or three magistrates. Both categories of judicial officers were expected to have the qualifications prescribed for a minister. There is no reference in the *Arthasatra* to a hierarchy of courts or to appeals from the decisions of a lower court to a higher one. An appeal could always be made to the king.

There shall be established a bench of three judges[7] who shall hold court at frontier posts, sub-district quarters, and provincial headquarters. The judges shall be learned in dharma and have the qualifications of a minister. They shall judge (civil) cases arising from disputes between two parties. Judges shall be fined and removed from offices if they act against dharma. A bench of three magistrates (pradeshtr), each of the rank of minister, shall be responsible for the suppression of anti-social activities.

The king sat in his court to administer justice. The *Arthasatra*[8] says "when in the court, the king shall never cause his petitioners to wait to the door". *Amatyas* were appointed in the courts. The *Arthasastra* says that the "*Amatya* (officers) purified by religious test, should be employed in civil and criminal courts. Civil or *Dharmasthiya*[9] courts were established in the cities of *Sangrahana* (in the midst of a collection of ten villages), *Droanamukha* (in the centre of four hundred villages), *Sthaniya* (in the centre of eight hundred villages), and at places where districts met i.e., at *janapada-sandhi, and* consisted of three *Dharmasthas* (judges versed in the sacred law) and three *Amatyas*. A criminal or *Kantakasodhana* court consisted of three *Amatyas,* or three *Pradeshtris.*

The statement of the *Kautilya Arthasastra* regarding the employment of *Amatyas* as the executive and judicial officers of the realm, is confirmed by the classical writers. Strabo, for example, observes, "the seventh caste consists of counsellors and assessors of the king". To these persons belong the office of state, tribunals of justice, and the whole administration of affairs.

The *adhyakshas* (magistrates) had charge also of the hunters, and have the power of rewarding or punishing those who merit either.

JUDICIAL ADMINISTRATION OF MAURAYAN RULERS

At the head of the judiciary, stood the king himself. Besides the royal court there were special tribunals of justice both in cities (nagrara) and country parts (janapada) presided over by *Vyavaharika Mahamatras* and *Rajukas* respectively. Greek writers refer to judges who listened to cases of foreigners. Petty cases in villages were decided by the headmen and the village elders. Punishments were very severe. But the rigours of judicial administration were sought to be mitigated by Asoka who meted out equal justice to all and instituted the system of itinerant *Mahamairas* to check maladministration in the outlying provinces. The judicial business of villages was carried on by the *Gramikas, Gramabhojakas* or *Ayuktas* who were assisted by the village elders.

Asoka gave adequate freedom to the *Rajukas* so that they could perform their duty fearlessly. Asoka granted a respite of three days to condemned man laying in prison under death sentence. Hulizch pointed out that the king Asoka used to proclaim an amnesty to criminals at almost every anniversary of his coronation.

CONTENTS OF THE PLAINT

Kautilya says that in the plaint should be entered, year, season, month, fortnight, day, documents (to be relied upon), the court (in which the plaintiff is lodged), the amount of debt, country, villages, caste, family names, occupation of the plaintiff and defendant together with the relationship in which they stood to each other. *Katyayanasmrti, Yajnavalkyasmrti, Mitakshara* and *Apararka* also require such contents in the plaint.

CRIME[5] AND MAINTENANCE OF LAW AND ORDER

According to Kautilya the suppression of crimes and the maintenance of law and order were the foremost duty of the king. He has called these anti-social elements as *Kantakas* or thorns in the body politic of the empire. The weeding out of these thorns, *Kantakasodhana*, ie., the suppression of criminals and other anti-social elements, was a basic function of the state. The *Arthasastra* devotes the entire fourth Book to this topic. The general condition of law and order then prevailing in the country as a whole was very good. Megasthenes has commented "there was rarity of law suits among Indians. They are not litigious. Witnesses and seals are unnecessary when a man makes a deposit. Their houses are unguarded". A general sense of law and order was, however, consistent with and perhaps maintained by a severe Penal Code.

The *Pradesikas* were the principal police officers, whose duty was to investigate the crimes committed in the region within their jurisdiction. All crimes were properly investigated and a great emphasis was placed on the thoroughness of the investigation in the case of major crimes.

JUDICIAL ADMINISTRATION (GUPTA PERIOD)

Chandragupta II actively set about to establish an ideally efficient system of administration. One important measure which he adopted in order to strengthen his hold on the empire was the appointment of his kith and kin as heads of provincial administrations.

JUSTICE

The great achievements of the Gupta period were promoted by a government which maintained peace over most of northern India for two hundred years and which, by the standards punishment of most early empires, was remarkably mild. The legal system was exceptionally mild, and the death penalty was not imposed even for the most serious crimes, and that subjects of the empire could move freely about the country without the need of passports or permits.

Schools of lawyers produced new dharmasastras, of which the most important is the pseudepigraphion ascribed to the Upanishadic sage Yajnavalkya, which formed the basis of the Hindu family law in most of India until it was supplanted by legislation in the 1950s. In Buddhism, the Yogachara school emerged, the starting point of the many developments in the Buddhism of later times in India, Tibet and China.

The Smriti law of the Gupta Age developed new rules about slavery as it existed in the preceding period. Adultery ranks among the lesser sins which should be expiated by the performance of appropriate penances. Only in extreme cases, as when a woman commits adultery with a Shudra or other low caste man, or has conceived or borne a child, or attempts to kill her husband, is she to be abandoned altogether. The records of the Gupta Age point to the continuance of some of the above ideas and practices.

The Smritis of the Gupta Age followed the older law in prescribing a life of vows and fasts as well as of renunciation for the widow and allowing her to inherit her husband's property. But Sankhas and Angiras as well as Harita strongly urge her to sacrifice herself on her husband's pyre.

In the society of Vatsyayana's time public opinion permitted a widow to live with a man of her choice; but she never enjoyed the social status of a wedded wife.

LAW AND JUSTICE UNDER HARSHA

The *Kadambari* speaks of the royal palace as having a court of justice where the judges (dharmadhikarins) sat on high cane seats. Law and justice in the age of Harsha were carried out along the well established lines but for a few innovations. The *Pramatara,* for example, figures only in post-Gupta inscriptions. Devahuti believes that he was probably associated with law and justice and explained the Dharmasastra to the king. Other court procedures point to a continuity of tradition. Bana refers to law courts and *adhikaranas.* Harsha's grants use the well-known legal terminology with regard to land rights.

As the executor of justice the king was the highest court of appeal but his legislative powers were always limited. Dharmasastra literature, customs of the land, usages of vocational groups, ratiocination, and the opinion of the learned were considered to be the sources of law. When all failed to solve the problem, the king was required to exercise his own judgment in accordance with the sources. He was, moreover, expected to be easily accessible and, as a judge, to possess restraint.

Some designations mentioned in apparently describe police duties. The term *danda,* with military, judicial or police connotations, is used in the latter sense in the *Harshacharita.* The *Dussadhasadhanikas* were probably police officers who were expected to perform those duties which were regarded as difficult (such as arresting hardened criminals). The words *sancharaka,* 'messenger', and *sarvagatah,* "one who could reach anywhere", indicate the presence of a confidential courier service which kept the king informed of public opinion, criticism, etc. Many palce guards are described as *dandadharas, vetragrahis,* etc. in the *Harshacharita.* Inscription refer to *chatas* and *bhatas* who most likely performed police duties. *Harshacharita* mention *chara-bhatas* as soldiers in the vanguard of the infantry.

In the *Harshacharita* a reference is also made of jails. On special occasions prisoners were released from jails before the expiry of their term. Writing about the judicial processes Yuan Chwang says:

"As the government is honestly administered and the people live together on good terms the criminal class is small. The statue law is sometimes violated and plots made against the sovereign; when the crime is brought to light the offender is imprisoned for life; he does not suffer any corporal punishment, but alive and dead he is not treated as member of the community (lit, as a man)."

REFERENCES

1. **यो दण्डयान्दण्डयेद्राजा सम्यग्वध्यांश्रव घातयेत्।**
इष्टं स्यात्क्रतुभिस्तेन समाप्तवरदक्षिणैः॥359॥ - yaj. 1.359.
इति सश्रि्चन्त्य नृपतिः क्रतुतुल्यफलं पृथक्।
व्यवहारान्स्वयं पश्येत्सभ्यैः परिवृतोऽन्वहम्॥360॥
इत्येवमुक्तप्रकारेण क्रतुतुल्यं फलं दण्डयदण्डने, स्वर्गादिनाशं चादण्डय दण्डने स्म्याग्विचिन्त्य पृथक्पृथग्वर्णादिक्रमेण, सभ्यैर्वच्यमाण्उलक्षणैः परिवृतः, प्रतिदिनं व्यवहारान्वचयमाणमार्गेण दृष्टादृष्टपरिज्ञानार्थ राजा स्वयं पश्येत्॥360। - yaj. 1. 360.

2. Narda, Yajnavalkya smriti II 30
3. Manu VIII 1-2
4. Yajnavalkya smriti II.1
5. Sukra Nitisara 14.5 114-117.
6. Sacred Books of East Vol. 36 P. 238
7. Kautilya III-1
8. Kautilya III-1 56.57. 1-1
9. Kautilya 14. 18.1
10. Kautilya 56-57. 1.1

BIBLIOGRAPHY

1. **Dr. Kailash Khanna** - History of Ancient India - p. 165
2. **Jha Vijendranarayana** - History of Anicient India - pp. 209-10.
3. **Gupt Shivkumar** - History of Anicient India - pp.287-289.
4. **Sharma Rita** - Anicient India - p. 190.
5. **Pandey Dr. Rajbali** - Indtrduction to Indian History- p. 99.
6. **Chander** - Chandragupt Maurya and His period- p. 203
7. **Chander** - Chandragupt Maurya and His period- p. 214
8. **Pandit Bhagvati Prasad** - 'Ashoka'- pp. 97-99
9. **Kachru Jivalal** - History of India - pp. 78-79.
10. **Gupt Shivkumar** - History of Ancient India - p. 287
11. **Gupt Shivkumar** - History of Ancient India - p. 289
12. **Rakshi Bhanu Singh Nahar** - Hindu Bharat (Hindi) Kitab Mahal Prabashan Allabad.
13. **Radha Krishna Choudhary** - Political & cultural histor of Ancient India (Hindi), Bharti Prakashan.
14. **Rajbali Pandey** - Introduction to Indian History, Hindi Prachar Lustakalya, 1954.

(All in Hindi)

5

Crimes and Punishments in Ancient India

5

CRIMES AND PUNISHMENTS IN ANCIENT INDIA

"If the king does not inflict punishment on those worthy to be punished, the stronger would roast the weaker like a fish on a spit"

- Manu Smriti

Vedic India provides glimpse of a society, not bound by rigid caste system, not fragmented by religious dogmas and the mental faculty not dwarfed by narrowness and therefore crimes were very few and simple like theft of animal stock, breaking into house, mutilating a part of body etc. Many acts which today tentamount to offence were ignored and were not taken any cognizance. Today, there is endless list of offences. Even smoking in public places, calling a person by his nick name, passing a comment on a girl, are treated as offence and actionable. Even Dowry cases relating to harassment or causing death to a married woman for dowry have assumed an alarming proportion in metro cities of India. In Delhi the central Jail Tihar is getting over one thousand new inmates annally necessiating a separate ward called (sass Bhau ward).

*

Saas-Nanad Ward in Tihar Jail

ANCIENT INDIA

In earlier or prevedic period the principle of "blood for blood" and "life for life" was followed. A killer must be killed and a person found guilty of mutilating, be dealt with likewise. During vedic period a more humanitarian, approach was made and the evaluation of human life was done in term of material wealth. The epithet "satadaya" i.e. "one, the price of whose blood was one hundred cows or (coins)" shows that the system of wergild (vairadeya) or blood money was probably in force. Theft, burglary, robbery, and cattle lifting were the principal crimes which were strongly dealt with by the administration. The debtor was punished with a servitude to the creditor and was bound by the creditor to a post to bring pressure on him for payment.

In later Vedic period the crime graph arose with the development of civilization. many a cases of crime belonged to the theft of livestock eg. cows, bulls etc. and the culprit had to return 4 cows for stealing 1 cow[1]. Among the other crimes enumerated are theft, robbery, adultery, incest, abduction, killing of man. Killing of cow, slaying of brahmana, drinking intoxicating liquor, treachery, etc. wer puishable by death, Petty offences were left to "village judges". The law was also very clear on the question of inheritance of property, ownership of land, etc. The father's property was to be inherited by sons alone. The daughters could inherit it only if she was the only child or there were no male issues. Tying the criminal to a stake was also a common form of punishment. Fine or payment of penalty in terms of money or externment from the kingdom were the other forms of punishment. What is particularly remarkable that some times punishment was awarded in common places like rural community centre (Chaupal) in the presence of village people just to create panic against committing such crimes.

Offences Punishable at the Level of King

The king's court would deal the following cases of offence:[2] (i) transgressions of the king's commandments and obedience to his injuctions (ii) grants of towns, (iii) dissensions among the constituent elements (such as ministers) of the State, the duties and breaches thereof among heretics, followers of the Veda, corporations (of merchants) and groups (iv) dispute between father and son (v) neglect of prescribed penances (vi) abstraction of gifts made to worthy persons, (vii) the wrath of hermits, (viii) sinful confusion of castes the other binds of offences. Where force is the principal element (termed as Sahasas) have been mentioned as homicide, robbery, rape, etc., vakparushya (defamation and abuse) and dandaparushya (hurt of various kind), attracted severe punishment.

FORMS OF PUNISHMENTS

Award of punishments depended on motive, sex, nature of offence, time and place, etc. Punishments such as banishment, death, impalement, in lieu of murder or cutting off a limb or theft, etc, branding of several marks on forehead, cutting off fingers, hands and feet (was common). In case of thieves and pickpockets, cutting off the limb sometimes, cutting off the tongue in the case of a sudra who abuses a brahmana or kshatriya or loudly repeats the Veda, or confiscation of property, etc were the other forms of punishment.

Petty offences in the village seem to have been left to the *gramyavadin* or village judge for disposal. It is curious that some time even a minor bodily defect such as the possession of bad nails, or the violation of a purely conventional practice was looked upon as a crime.

Eye witness were more important than informers. Ordeals were also looked upon as valid tests for uncommon guilt. The punishments for crimes were rather severe. If a thief was caught red-handed, death or the cutting of hands was a penalty; in milder causes, binding to posts and the return of stolen goods sufficed as punishment.

Civil Cases

A regards civil cases voluntary arbitration appears to be the earlier form of judicial procedure, in which the plaintiff (prasnin), the defendant (abhi prasnin), and the arbitrator or judge (prasnairvaka), figured. Witness was called Jnatri.

AGE OF NANDAS AND MAURYAS '600 B.C.' TO 100 B.C"

The Nanda dynasty was brought to end by Chandra - Gupta under the guidance of Chankya and Mauryas ruled the major part of India for several centuries. A strict panel code was followed particularly by Chandra Gupta and Crime rate was considerably low.

CHANDRAGUPTA - PENAL CODE

The criminal code was very harsh and was strictly administered to set an example for others and to deter them from doing wrong.

Common Crimes and Offences

Theft, murder, burglary, combinations to raise or depress prices, rape, defiant or violation of caste rules.

(i) short measure or false weights, (ii) the artisan who failed to keep his contract with his employer (iii) the physician who caused the death of his patient by his lack of skill (iv) the official who swindled the state or took bribes, (v) the conspirator who contemplated treason against the king.

Punishments

Crippling one by cutting off one's limb or deforming it was punished the same way and in addition accused was remderd one- handed man Deforming a craftsmen's hand or an eye, was sentenced to death.

There were eighteen kinds of tortures including seven of whipping. The evidence of respectable person was relied upon. Punishment was very severe, even for small offences like evasion of govt. taxes, giving false evidence, causing injury to artisans, ordinary theft, etc., the body was mutilated.

Some other notable features were :

1. In the absence of solid evidence none would be arrested suspiciously on the expiry of three days from the commitment of the crime.
2. Abetting for committing the crime was punishable.
3. Storage of goods for sale at unauthorized place caused its forfieture.

4. If a businessman was harmed with a major theft, the ten nearly villages had to pay tax to compensator the loss.
5. Pick-pockets were punished rigorously.
6. For simple crimes/offence, fine or penalty as mentioned by Kautilya was imposed depending upon the kind of offences which were graded as under :
   - Coorusahas dand (48 to 96 coins)
   - Madhyamsahas dand (200 to 500 coins).
   - Uttamsohas dond (500 to 100 coins).

PERIOD OF ASHOKA

Ashoka continued the same penal code initially. However having won the infamous Kalinga war where in around 1 lac people were slain, he adopted Buddhism & penal code was relaxed and was made compassionate reducing its severity Mahamatras were sent to different cities & towns to see that the people are not sent behind bars without any evidence or crime or not harassed without reason.

A rock Pillar addict reads, *"For this purpose has this prescript been written here, viz. that the city judges may devote themselves at all time (this, viz.) that men may not be put in fetters without reason or be harassed without reason. In addition, for this purpose I shall send out, every five years, Mahamatras who will not be harsh, not fierce, but of gentle action, and who, bearing this matter in mind, will carry out this too as my instructions are. Moreover, from Ujjayini too, the Prince, for the same purpose, will send out similar persons every three years. In the same manner also from Takshasila.....*"

The office of the Dhamma-mahamatras was created by Ashoka thirteen years after his coronation as he states in Rock Edict V which sets forth their duties in some details. The Dhamma-mahamatras were to establish and promote Dhamma among all sects in the land. They reviewed all sentences awarded by courts and mitigated or remitted them after taking into account the particular circumstances of each case.

The city was divided into four parts, each headed by a *sthanika* who was subordinate to the *nagarika,* the chief city official. *Gopas,* who were under the *sthankas,* supervised 10 to 20 or 40 families of city residents. Ashoka annually proclaimed an amnesty. He also introduced a three-day respite of the carrying out of death sentences "to enable the convicted person's relatives to appeal for his life to be spared". The Mauryas attached great importance to legal procedure and declared that their aim was to make justice prevail in both court trials and the meting out of punishment.

The *Rajukas* performed judicial duties. Asoka asked them to perform their duties confidently and fearlessly and desired that the care of these officers should resemble that of "an intelligent nurse for the child in her charge".

GUPTA AGE

Gupta period witnessed a lenient penal code. Capital punishment was avoided even in serious offences, except in case of mutiny or treasons. Fine or penalty amount depended upon the kind of offence. Corporal punishment or physical torture was refrained to. In selected cases the guilty was sentenced in full public view at common places in order to drive right message to the people and to deter them from committing such crimes.

VARDHAN PERIOD

Vardhan Empire was the biggest & the mightiest covering a large Chunk of India. The judicial system followed there in would influence the neighboring kingdoms as well. The panel code was tightened and the following punishments/ sentences were awarded:-

i. life imprisonment for treason.

ii. Mutilation of ear, nose, arms or legs for rape, kidnapping, forced adultery & also to the person found traitor.

iii. Externment from kingdom for serious offences.

iv. Fine or financial punishment for civil offences.

v. One of distinguishing features was that the truthfulness & facts of case were testified through the ordeals of water, fire, poison etc.

For offences against social morality, and disloyal or unfilial conduct, the punishment was to cut off the nose, or an ear, or a hand, or a foot, or to banish the offender to another country or into the wilderness. Other offences would be atoned for by money payment.[1]

Kadambari Bana a famous work of Vardhan period makes a reference to *divyas* or ordeals somewhat differently they are also mentioned by Yuan Chwang:[3] These are by water, by fire, by weighing, and by poison. In the water ordeal the accused is put in one sack and a stone in another, then the two sacks are connected and thrown into a deep stream; if the sack containing the stone floats, and the other sinks, the man's guilt is proven. The fire ordeal required the accused to kneel and tread on hot iron, to take it in his hand and lick it; if he is innocent he is not hurt, but he is hurt, if he is guilty. In the weighing ordeal the accused is weighed against a stone; and if the latter is the lighter the charge is false, if otherwise it is true. The poison ordeal requires that a cut is made in the right hand leg of a man, and poisons are put into the leg, and if the man is innocent he survives, and if not the poison takes effect.[4]

CHOLA CRIMINAL LAW

In the Chola period, *Rajadroham* or treason was considered a most heinous offence. For such offences, punishments were naturally very severe.[5] Most offences were generally punished by fines.

Offences like man-slaughter and murder were often punished with the maintainance of a perpetual lamp in the temple. The inscriptional evidences show that severe punishment was not given for accidental death. But the Chinese writer of the early 13th century Chau-Ju-Kua speaking about the Chola empire, observes: "When any one among the people is guilty of an offence, one of the court ministers punishes him; if the offence is light, the culprit is tied to a wooden frame and given fifty, seventy, or up to one hundred blows with a stick. Heinous crimes are punished with decapitation or by being trampled to death by an elephant.

CONCLUSION

Though a distinction was made between civil and criminal disputes among the eighteen titles of law, it appears that the set of rules and procedures in both were same, the same courts tried both kinds of disputes and not as in modern times. The law of the texts was moderated suitably by common sense and reason.

REFERENCES

1. **The Vedic Age,** E.D.R.C. Majumolar Bhartiya Vidhya Bhawan, Bombay, p. 438, 1965.
2. **Narda Smriti**

3. **On Yuan Chwang's Travels in India** (A Translation of Hsuan-tsang's His-Yu-Chi), by T. Watters.
4. **Goyal, S. 1992,** History and Historiography of the Age of Harsha, Jodhpur : Kusumanjali Book World, pp. 284-85.
5. **T.V. Mahalingam,** South Indian Polity, University of Madras, 1955, p.201.

* H.T. News

BIBLIOGRAPH

1. **Dr. Kailash Khanna** - History of Ancient India - p. 165
2. **Jha Vijendranarayana**-History of Ancient India-pp.209-10
3. **Gupt Shivkumar** - History of Ancient India - pp. 287-289, pp. 78.
4. **Sharma Rita** - Ancient History, p. 190.
5. **Pandey Dr. Rajbali** - Introduction to Indian History - p. 99.
6. **Chander** - Chandargupt Maurya and his period, p.203.
7. **Chander** - Chandargupt Maurya and his period, p.214.
8. **Pandit Bhagvati Prasad** - 'Ashoka' - pp. 97-99.
9. **Kachru Jivalal** - History of India, pp. 78-79.
10. **Gupt Shivkumar** - History of Ancient India, p. 287.
11. **Gupt Shivkumar** - History of Ancient India, p. 289.
12. **Rakshi Bhanu Singh Nahar** - Hindu Bharat (Hindi), Kitab Mahal Prakashn, Allahabad.
13. **Radha Krishna Choudhary** - Political & Cultural history of Ancient India (Hindi), Bharti Prakashan.
14. **Rajbali Pandey** - Introduction to Indian History, Hindi Prachar Pustakalaya, 1954.

(All in Hindi)

6

Kinds and Setup of Courts

6

KINDS AND SETUP OF COURTS

*

One can discern that there has been consistent growth, changes and revamping in the kinds and setup of courts, right from vedic period, to answer the needs of the time and to keep paca with socio-economic condition as well as political spectrum. In vedic period as well as later vedic period, India comprised of several kingdoms and Janpadas ruled by the individual kings and monarchs.

Nearly, 90-95% of the population was inhabited in villages and cities (Nagaras) were very few. As such the setup of courts was also synchronised accordingly. In the capital city, the court was headed by the king himself and he was assisted by his amatyas and purohits knowing dharma. The Judicial set up was, however decentralized in the sense that serious cases were entertained in the royal court while the common ones of civil as well criminal nature were decided by village sabha & *smiti*, both were powerful bodies enjoined with *administration* as well as judicial function.

The village sabha was headed by Gram Vadini. The executive body of Sabha consisting of the representatives of groups of families which would meet and handover the case to a panel of three members of the executive body, well versed in legal matters. The sabha was autonomous in its functioning.

King's Court

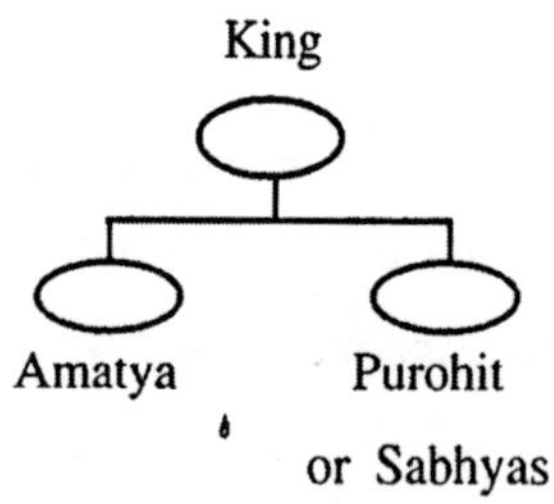

Rural Area Courts

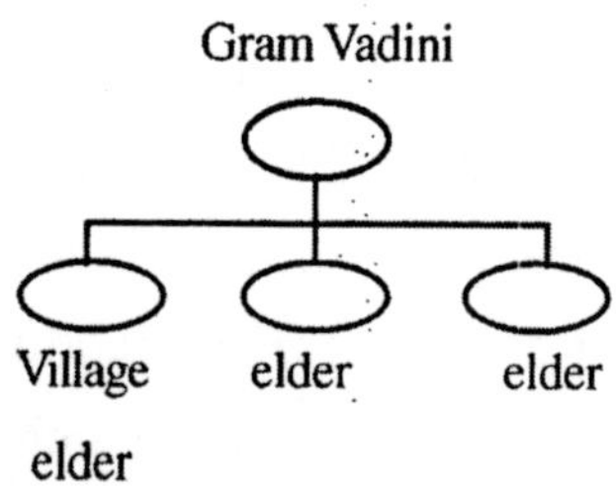

Later Vedic Period

In Later Vedic period some kingdoms expanded and grew stronger with more & more territories got added. Nagaras (cities), new Janpadas devleoped as such Judge's court were set up in important cities also. Such courts were headed by chief judge, associated with three sabhyas. The rural courts were of three kinds :

(i) Kula

(ii) Shreni and

(iii) Gana

Kula - an association of families & kins-men, and Shreni was the association of person of different castes but practising the same craft. Gana was a federation of all these associations and comprised the whole village republic[1]. The Kula, Shreni and Gana functioned as courts of law- subordinate to the kings court and to the king himself as final court of appeal.

However, the judges there in, had the approval from the king who was also empowered to make any changes there in and also to constitute special court for prompt justice to the people. The study of contemporary literature shows that many a times spies were deployed to investigate the case and to report the facts to the king. Special care was exercised to ensure that an innocent person does not get punishment and a serious view was taken in case the higher court lets of the accused person and the judge of the trial court was subjected to intensive seruting to see if any favouritism or leniency was shown to the either party.

King's Court

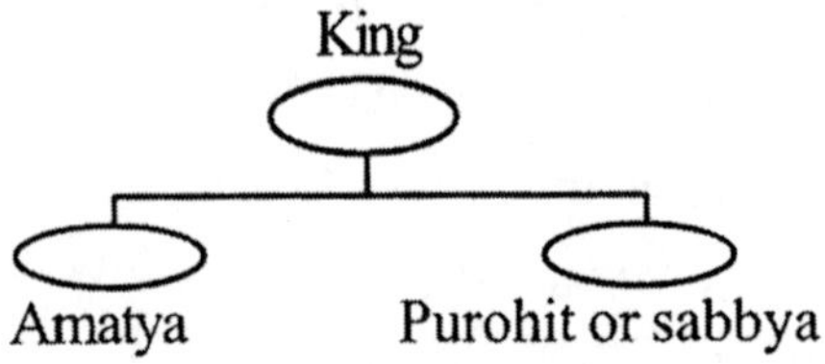

Judges' Court

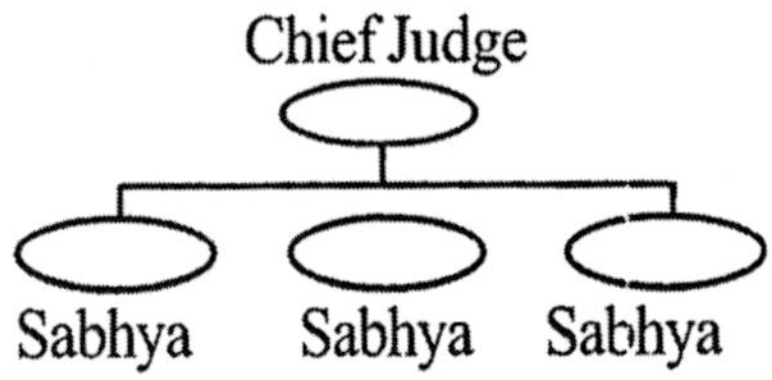

Rural court

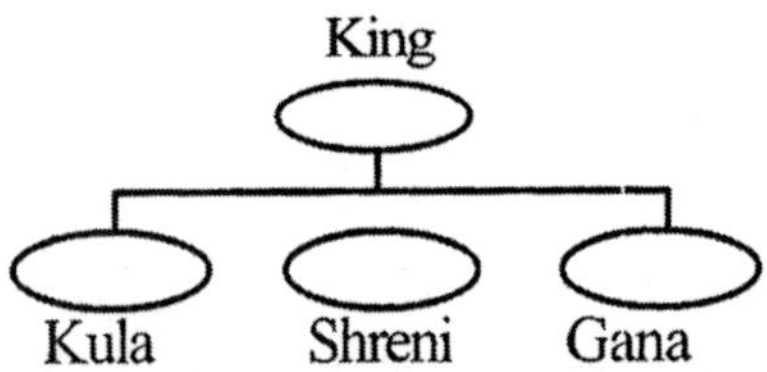

WHAT SMRITIS & DHARM SASHTRAS SAY?

During Mauryan period various Hindu scriptures i.e. Gautam smiriti, Narada smirit; Yajnavlka, Brahspati, Manu smrities came up containing regulations on various aspects of social life like education, marriage, worshiping, employment as apprentice including jurisprudence. The socio-economic structure also developed, more cities came up therewith, the mighty empire of Maurya kings covered almost the whole India.

According to Brhaspati[1], a Court of Justice was of four kinds.

1. **Pratishthita,** one established in a fixed place such as a town.
2. **Apratishtita,** not fixed in one place, but moving from place to place as on a circuit.
3. **Mudrita,** the court of a judge appointed by the king, who is authorized to use the royal seal, and
4. **Sasita,** i.e., the court in which the king himself presides.

OTHER COURTS MENTIONED IN SMIRITIS

Other tribunals were also recognized in the *Smrtis* and digests. Yajnavalkya[2] and Narada[3] state that law-suits may be decided by village councils (kula), corporations (*Shreni*), assemblies (*puga* in Yaj and *gana* in Nar.), the judges appointed by the king and the king himself, each later one being superior to each preceding one. The first three were practically arbitration tribunals like the modern *panchayats.* The king was the highest court of appeal and next to him was the court of the judges appointed by him. Bhrgu says that there are ten tribunals common to all men, viz., the village people, the assembly of the citizens of the capital, *gana, shreni,* men learned in the four Vedas, the *vargins, kulas, kulikas,* judges, and the king himself.

SET UP AND KINDS OF COURT

IN MAURYAN PERIOD

For the administration of justice, there were two sets of courts besides the village tribunals that dealt with petty cases under the guidance of the headman and elders; these were called the Dharmasthiya and Kantakasodhana. The Civil or *Dharmasthiya* courts were established in the cities at Sangrahana (in the midst of a collection of ten villages), *Droanamukha* (in the centre of four hundred villages), *Sthaniya* (in the centre of eight hundred villages), and at place where districts met i.e., at *janapada-sandhi,* and consisted of three *Dharmasthas* (judges versed in the sacred law) and three *Amatyas.* A criminal or *Kantakasodhana* court consisted of three *Amatyas,* or three *Pradeshtris.*

The king was the head of justice-the fountainhead of law- and all matters of grave consequences were decided by him. There were special courts in the cities and villages presided over by the *pradesika, mahamatas* and *rajukas.* In all important cities and headquarters, at least one court and one police head office was set up. Petty cases in the villages were settled by the village elders in their *panchayats.* In civil cases the Hindu code of law, as envisaged in the *sastras,* was administered. The evidence of respectable persons was relied upon.

The Dharmasthiya courts were presided over by three dharmasthas learned in sacred law and three amatyas, and there were courts in all important cities and other convenient centres; rules were laid down about circumstances which rendered agreements void, and about procedure in court-plea, counterplea and rejoinder. The main heads of civil law dealt with 1) marriage and dowry including divorce, 2) inheritance 3) houses, house-sites and disputes regarding boundaries and water-rights, and trespass, 40 debt, 5) deposits, 6) serfs, 7) labour and contract, 8) sale 9) violence 10) abuse, 11) assault, 12) gaming and miscellanea.

In many respects Kautilya is seen to lay down rules that alter and liberalise the precepts of the ancient texts, and in his hands the exposition of the whole subject is more rational and progressive than orthodox and conservative. In the absence of witnesses the ordeal was resorted to. Punishments were carefully graded and executed by royal authority. They included fines, imprisonment, whipping and death with or without torture. There must have been in existence also caste panchayats and guild courts which regulated the affairs of communities and professions and deals with disputes among them in the first instance.

MAURAYAN PERIOD - SETUP OF COURTS

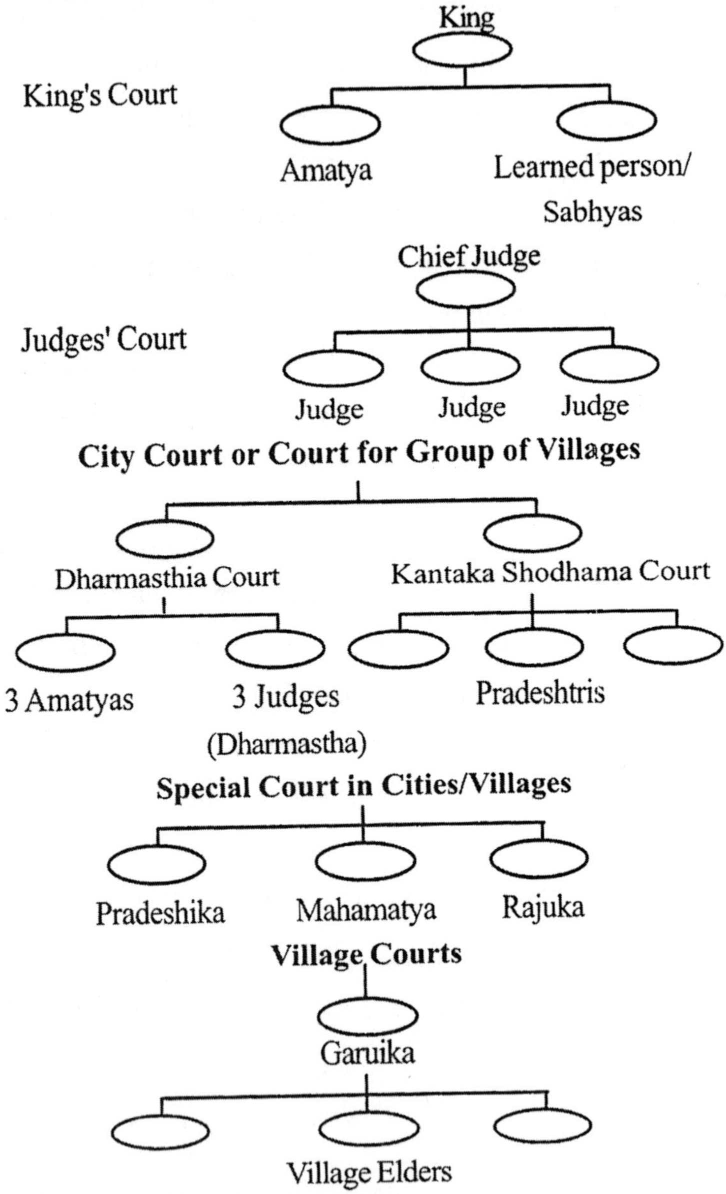

KANTAKASODHANA - COURTS

The Kantakasodhana (removal of thorns) courts were presided over by three pradeshtris or three amatyas. The basis of the distinction between these courts and the dharmasthiya courts is nowhere clearly explained. The suggestion has been offered that while the dharma courts dealt with disputes brought before them by the parties and strictly corresponded to civil courts, in the kantakasodhana courts the actions started on the initiative of the executive. This looks plausible in the light of modern juristic ideas, but it may well be doubted if the distinction between the two sets of courts was so simple and clear-cut. For instance, while assault and hurt were generally dealt with by the dharma courts, assault ending in manslaughter was reserved for the kantakasodhana. The truth seems to be that the kantakasodhana courts were a new type introduced to meet the growing need of an increasingly complex social economy, and to implement the decisions of a highly organized bureaucracy on all matters that were being brought under their control and regulation for the first time and were unknown to the old legal system. These courts were special tribunals which followed a more summary procedure than the regular dharma courts that dealt with vyavahara as developed in the tradition of the dharmasastras;

their functions were only quasi-judicial, and their methods and more in common with those of a modern police force than of a judiciary.

The aim of K.S. Courts was to protect the state and people from baneful actions of antisocial persons, the thorns (kantaka) of society. There resorted to the use of spies for the detection of such activity and o torture for the extortion of confessions. The merchant who used short measure or false weights, the artisan who failed to keep his contract with his employer, the physician who caused the death of his patient by his lack of skill, the official who swindled the state or took bribes, and the conspirator who contemplated treason against the king – were all dealt with by these courts. Theft, murder, burglary, combinations to reaise or depress prices, ape, defiant violation of caste rule and so on, are also among the offences bought before these courts. In these courts we may well recognize another innovation of Kautilya, based on foreign model and calculated to strengthen the power of the monarch and the position of the new bureaucracy.

ASHOKA – THE GREAT

Ashoka maintained the same framework of polity but created some new offices for the spread of Dharma and sought to impart by example and precept an earnest moral tone to the entire system of administration. Megastanes records that "There were few crimes; murders and thefts were almost unknown, people seldom locked their doors and the security of life and property was guaranteed by the state".

The status of the rajukas was subordinate to that of the pradesika. The duties of the yukta largely comprised secretarial work and accounting.

There was an intermediate level of administration between the district level and that of the village. The unit here was formed by a group of five or ten villages. The two important officials of this unit were the sthanika and the gopa.

VILLAGE ADMINISTRATION

Village (grama) was the smallest unit of administration. The head of a village was known as gramika who was assisted by gramaviddhas or 'villages elders'. Gramika was not a paid servant; he was elected by the people.

As head of state, the Mauryan ruler, judging by the inscriptions, could personally appoint officials of any rank, The VIIth Major Pillar Edict, for example, refers to the appointment of dharmamahamatras, rajukas etc. The Vth Major Rock Edict reads; *"In the past there were no mahamatras responsible for the Dharma, but after a lapse of thirteen years I have appointed Dharmamahamatras".*

The 1st Special Edict, in which *anusamyana* occurs, deals with the sending of mahamatras by the emperor to cheek the actions of the local authorities. The edict reads; *"For this purpose has this rescript been written here, viz. that the City Judges may devote themselves at all times (this, viz.) that men may not be put in fetters without reason or be harassed without reason. In addition, for this purpose I shall send out, every five years, Mahamatras who will not be harsh, not fierce, but of gentle action, and who, bearing this matter in mind, will carry out his too as my instructions are. Moreover, from Ujjayini too, the Prince, for the same purpose, will send out similar persons every three years. in the same manner also from Takshasila...."*

The Mauryas attached great importance to legal procedure and declared that their aim was to make justice prevail in both court trials and the meting out punishment.

The *Rajukas* performed judicial duties. Asoka asked them to perform their duties confidently and fearlessly and desired that the care of these officers should resemble that of "an intelligent nurse for the child in her charge".

The *dharmamahamatras* reviewed all sentences awarded by courts and mitigated or remitted them after taking into account the particular circumstances of each case.

Nagala-Viyohalakas (Nagara Vyavaharikas) – they administered justice in the city.

AGE OF THE GUPTAS

During the Gupta period the king governed without decapitation or other corporal punishments. Criminals were simply fined lightly or heavily, according to the circumstances of each case. Even in cases of repeated attempts of wicked rebellion they only had their right hand cut off.

SET UP OF COURTS

Justice was often administered by the sovereign himself or by a high official at the centre of the provinces. Judges at the head-quarters of a distinct had apparently the assistance of the chief *Seths* and *Kayasthas* of the locality, representatives of the vocational and official classes in villages, justice was administered by royal officials with the help of the members of the village council or assembly. In certain cases the assembly alone sat in judgment and passed sentence. Special courts of self-governing corporations are also alluded to in literature. The jury system, according to some authorities, is found to have been in full swing at least in southern India. Judicial methods included trial by ordeal.

REFERENCES

1. सारस्तु व्यवहाराणां प्रतिज्ञा समुदाहृता।
   तद्धानौ हीयते वादी तरस्तामुत्तरो भवेत्॥6॥
   कुलानि श्रेणंयश्चैव गणाश्चाधिकृतो नृपः।
   प्रतिष्ठा व्यवहाराणां गुर्वेभ्यस्तुत्तरोत्तरम्॥7॥ *- Narda 1.7*
2. नृपेणाधिकृताः पूगाः श्रेणयोऽघ कुलानि च।
   पूर्वे पूर्वे गुरु श्रेयं व्यवहारविघौ नृणाम्॥30॥ - *Yaj. 2.30.*

BIBLOGRAPHY

1. Jha Vijenolranarayan - History of Ancient India, pp. 209-10. (Hindi)
2. Pandey Dr. Rajboli - Introduction of Indian History, p. 99 (Hindi)
3. Chander Chandargupta - Maurya & His period, p. 214 (Hindi).
4. Gupta Shivkumar - History of Ancient India, p.287 (Hindi)
5. Rakshi Bhanu Singh Nahar - Hindu Bharat (Hindi) Kitab - Mahal Prakashan, Allabahad

* H.T. News

7

Witness, Evidence and Ordeals in Ancient India

7

WITNESS, EVIDENCE AND ORDEALS IN ANCIENT INDIA

Witness and evidence form an important component in modern judicial system. So was the case in ancient India also. In case of denial by the other party, the burden of proof was on the plaintiff. Yajnavalkya[1], Narada, Brhaspati and others say that means of proof are two fold, human and divine, and that documents, witnesses and possession are the human means of proof, while the ordeals of balance and others are divine means. The ordeals are to be resorted to only when none of the other option is available, otherwise, the king (or judge) has to accept human means, and not divine. According to Brhaspati "witnesses are superior to inference (circumstantial evidence), a document is superior to witnesses, undisturbed possession for three generations is superior to all these".

WHAT IS AN ORDEAL?

An ordeal is a tedious and painful exercise given to an accused to test his innocence or the truthfulness of statement where in use of fire or water, or poison etc. is made and it is assumed that fire water or poison will not harm the person if he is truthful. Religious environment is created by chanting Vedic mantras and invoking gods who are believed to help the accused, if he is truthful and innocent. The ordeals mentioned in Kadambri are as under.

These are by water, by fire, by weighing, and by poison. In the water ordeal, the accused is put in one sack and a stone in another, then the two sacks are connected and thrown into a deep stream; if the sack containing the stone floats, and the other sinks, the man's guilt is proven. The fire ordeal required the accused to kneel and read on hot iron, to take it in his hand and lick it; if he is innocent he is not hurt, but he will hurt if he is guilty. In the weighing ordeal the accused is weighted against a stone; and if the latter is lighter the charge is false, if otherwise it is true. The poison ordeal requires that the right hind leg a ram be cut off, and according to the portion assigned to the accused to eat, poisons are put into the leg, and if the man is innocent, he survives, and if not the poison takes effect.

In Smrities and Dharm sutras the ordeals are described as under :

1. Tula or dhata or balance

A balance was carefully prepared from a sacrificial tree. In the pan to the west, the sodhya should be placed and weighed against clay, bricks and stones placed in the other pan. Then traders or goldsmiths or braziers should examine the Balance and bring "ifdisa level and examine the balance and bring it on a level and examine the perfect horizontality of the beam of the balance by spilling a little water on the beam. When the person sitting in one pan is equal in weight to the materials in the other, a line should be drawn with chalk by the experts on the arch to show the exact position of the pans. Then the man is made to get down from the pan and he invokes the balance as stated in Yaj[2] II. 101-102. Then is again to be placed in the pan to the accompaniment of invocations (Nar. IV. 278-279). If the person goes up (ie is found lighter than what he formerly weighed) lie is declared innocent (Com. on Nar. IV. 283 and Dipakalika on Yaj. II. 102); if he weighs the same or goes down (ie weighs more) he is guilty.

2. Ordeal by fire

Nine circles with cowdung are to be drawn from west to east, they being, meant for different deities. In each circle kusa grass was to be spread and the person to be tested was to plant his feet on them; ghee was to be offered into fire 108 times. A blacksmith by birth should heat in fire a ball of iron weighing 50 palas (16 palas in the case of a weak man) and eight angulus in length till it becomes red-hot and emits sparks. The sodhya should stand in the first circle facing east. Having made red marks on all sides of the hands of the sodhya on which grains of rice have been rubbed, he (the judge) should palce seven leaves of the asvattha tree on them and also grains of rice and curds and should fasten round them threads. Then the judge should carry the red-hot iron piece by means of a pair of tongs and place it in the hands of the sodbtya {that are covered with leaves). Then the sodhya holding in both his hands the red-hot piece should walk from the first to the eighth circle not hurriedly but slowly and at ease. Having reached the 8th circle he should throw the red-hot iron piece on to the 9th circle. Then the judge should rub on the hands of the sodhya rice grains and when the latter shows no hesitation at the rubbing and no injury on his hand at the end of the day he is declared to be innocent. Yaj II. 107[3] provides that if the red-hot piece falls earlier or there is a doubt whether his hands are injured or not) or if he loses his footing or is burnt elsewhere than on the hands, he should again undergo the ordeal.

THE ORDEAL OF WATER

Having gone to a reservoir of water the judge should get erected on its bank a torana (an arch) as high as the ear of the sodhya on an even and cowdunged plot. He should offer worship to Varuna, to a bow of middling size and to three arrows with ṣandal paste, incense, lamp, flowers. A target is to be fixed at the distance of 150 hastes (cubits) from the torana. A post of some sacred tree is to be fixed in the water and a strong man of one of the three higher castes free from love or hatred for the sodhya is to stand in navel-deep water facing the east and holding the post. Then the judge is to make the sodhya stand in water, invoke the deities from Dharma to Durga, perform all the rites up to the placing of the writing on the head of sodhya. A kshtriya or a brahmana following the profession of arms who is of pure heart and has observed a fast should discharge, while standing near the root of the torana, three arrows at the target. The sodhya should invoke the water with a mantra. Then a young but swift man should run to the spot where the second arrow struck the ground, and stand their holding that arrow in his hand. Another swift man stands at the root of the torana whence the arrows were discharged. Then the judge claps his hands thrice. At the third clap the sodhya dives into the water seizing the thighs of the man standing in water and at the same time the swift, man near the arch runs at his best speed to place where the second arrow fell. The other man who holds the arrow starts off the moment the first runner reaches him and conies running to the arch. If he does not see the sodhya or sees only his head (ie. The back of the head) when he reaches the arch the sodhya is to be declared innocent; but if sees other parts of the head (such as the ear or nose etc) or if the sodhya floats to some part other than the one where he dived he is not innocent.

ORDEAL OF POISON

The poison to selected is saarnga (derived from the sranga plant) or vatsanabha (aconite) or haimavata (Nar. IV. 322)/ Poison was to be mixed with ghee thirty times as much. After invoking gods, Narada IV.[4] 326 states that the sodhya should eat the poison, should be kept in shade without food and guarded the rest of the day and if he discloses no signs of the effect of poison, should be declared innocent.

THE ORDEAL OF KOSA

The sodhya is made to worship the stem deities such as Rudra, Durga, Aditya. Then the judge asks the sodhya to invoke the consecrated water with the mantra 'satyena mabhiraksha' (Yaj 11.108) and makes him drink three handfuls of that water. The water may be that of the bath of the image of that god of which the sodhya is a devotee. If within fourteen days of taking the kosa ordeal the sodhya does not suffer any serious calamity due to the king's action or the act of God or does not fall seriously ill or does not lose by death his son or wife or other dear relative or his wealth, then he is to be declared innocent.

ORDEAL OF TANDULA (RICE GRAINS)

It is to be administered in charges of theft or disputes about debts or other monetary matters. On the preceding day grains of rice should be made white (ie, husked). The judge should perform all the rites on the previous day. The rice grains should be placed in an earthern vessel, exposed &, the sun, water of the bath of the Sun should be poured over them in the vessel and the vessel should be kept in that state the whole night. The next day in the morning the sodhya should swallow thrice the rice grains. He should be made to spit on a pippala or birch leaf. If blood is found mixed in his saliva he should be declared guilty.

ORDEAL OF TAPTAMASHA (Heated Piece of Gold)

In a vessel of copper, Iron-or ^lay sixteen angulas in diameter and four angulas deep, the judge should get twenty palas of ghee and oil poured and heat it to the boiling point. Then the judge should cast into it a golden piece weighing one mashaka (equal to five gunjas). The sodhya. should take out the heated golden piece with the thumb and the next two fingers. If he does not jerk his fingers or there is no scalded skin he should be declared to be innocent.

ORDEAL BY PHALA (Ploughshare)

A ploughshare of iron weighing twelve palas, eight angulas long should be made red-hot and the thief should be made to lick it once with his tongue. If he is not burnt he establishes his innocence; if otherwise, he is guilty.

SELECTION AND OPTION OF ORDEALS

Manu VIII. 14 mentions only two ordeals viz. the holding of fire (ie. Red-hot iron) in the hand or plunging in water, but Narada TV.25I states that Manu declared five kinds of ordeals. Narada IV. 252 mentions five ordeals such as balance, fire, water, poison and kosa (consecrated water). He also knew two more viz. taptamasha (IV. 343) and tandula (IV. 337).

Yajnavalkya[5] (II. 95) also mentions five ordeals such as balance, fire, water, poison and kosa (consecrated water). However, Yaj (11.22) and Nar. (II. 29) state that ordeals were to be resorted to only if no human evidence (witnesses, documents, possession) or circumstantial evidence was available. Nar. (II. 30) states that divine means of proof are to be resorted to when a transaction takes place in a forest, in a lonely place, at night, inside a house, in cases of sahasa and when a deposit is denied, etc. Nar. TV. 242 further states that divine proof could be resorted to when the chastity of women was in question , in theft and sahasa and in all cases of the denial of monetary liability.

The ordinary rule was that ordeals were to be administered to the defendant. But Yaj. II. 96 gives an option that any one of the two litigants may by mutual agreement undergo an ordeal and the other should agree to pay on defeat a fine or undergo physical punishment.

Making an offer to pay a fine or undergo corporal punishment is said to be sirshakastha or sirastha (Yaj. II.[6] 95) and Nar. (IV. 257)[6]. Yaj II. 95 prescribes that the ordeals of balance, fire poison and ware were to be prescribed in disputes of great value and not elsewhere and in II. 99 he says that all claims above 1000 panas (of copper) are to be regarded as of great value, but in charges of treason and of the committing of any one of the five grave sins (mahapatakas) any one of these four ordeals may be resorted to without regard to value and without any offer to pay fine on defeat. So also these four ordeals were to be offered to the defendant where the plaintiff offered to pay a fine on defeat. The ordeal of kosa was allowed in all claims whether of high value or low value or whether the plaintiff offered to pay a fine on defeat or not.

Yaj. II. 98 states that the ordeal of balance should be given to women, a minor (under 16), a very old person {above eighty years), the blind, the cripple, brahmanas and the diseased; the fire ordeal (ie., heated ploughshare and heated masa) to kshatriyas, water ordeal to vaisyas, poison to sudras.

Nar. IV. 335 assigns ordeals to the different varnas. Similarly, Nar IV. 256 prescribes that ordeals should not be undergone by those who are observing a vow, who are much distressed or who are performing austerities, and by women.

Yaj. 11.97 and Nar IV. 268[7], 320 prescribe that all ordeals are to be administered by the chief justice in the morning at sunrise or in the forenoon in the presence of the king, the sabhyas and brahmanas. Nar. IV. 254 states mat the fire ordeal be given in the rainy season, balance in the winter (sisira), water in summer, poison when the season is cool. Nar, IV. 259 prohibits water ordeal in the cold season, fire in summer, poison in the rainy season and balance while the wind blows violently. Nar. IV. 265 prescribes that the balance should be planted in the hall of justice or at the royal gate or near a temple or where four roads meet.

The Procedure Common to All Ordeals

In ordeals the chief justice is to do every thing at the king's bidding as the adhvaryu priest does in all sacrifices. He should observe a fast and the sodhya (person undergoing the ordeal to clear himself) is also to do the same. Both are to bathe in the morning and the sodhya was to have his wet clothes on. The Chief Judge is to invoke the gods to the accompaniment of music and to offer flowers, sandalwood paste and incense. He should fold his hands, face the east and invoke Dharma to be present at the ordeal (Dharma being the principal deity in ordeals) and assign places to different deities. All these deities are to be invoked with appropriated Vedic mantras. He should offer the several items of worship from arghya (water offered by way of honour) to ornament to Dharma (as the principal deity) and then to the subsidiary deities from Indra to Durga and then sandalwood paste, flowers, incense, lamp and naivedya to the deities from Dharma to Durga. The flowers for Dharma are to be red. Up to this *is* the work of the Chief Justice. Sacrificial priest should offer into fire in the four quarters 108 oblations of clarified butter, boiled rice and fuel sticks with syllable Om and the Gayatri and with Om and svaha at the end of each. Having written down on a leaf the subject matter for which the party is undergoing ordeal, the leaf should be placed on the head of the sodhya with the mantra, ***'the sun, the moon, the wind, fire, heaven and earth, waters, the heart, Yama, day and night, the two twilights and Dharma know the deeds of men'.***

REFERENCES

1. Yaj.2.29

योऽभियुक्तः परेतः स्यात्तभ्य रिक्थी तमुद्धरेत्।
न तत्र कारणं भुक्तिरागमेन विना कृता॥

Narda II.29.

क्रियापि द्विविधा प्रोक्ता मानुषी दैविकी तथा।
मानुषी लेख्यसाक्षिभ्यां धटादिर्देविकी स्मृता॥
दिवा कृते कार्यविधौ ग्रामेषु नगरेषु वा।
संभवे साक्षिणां चैव दिव्या न भवति क्रिया॥
अरण्ये निर्जने रात्रावन्तर्वेश्मनि साहसे।
न्यासस्यापह्नवे चैव दिव्या संभवति क्रिया॥

2. Yajya.II. 102,103

प्रतिमानसमीभूतो रेखीं कृत्वाऽवतारितः॥
'त्वं तुले सत्यधामासि पुरा देवैर्विनिर्मिता।
तत्सत्यं वद कल्याणि। संशयान्मां विमोचय॥
यद्यस्मि पापकृन्मातस्ततो मां त्वमघो नय।
शुद्धश्चेद् गमयोर्ध्वं मां तुलामित्यभिमन्ययेत्॥

Narda IV 278-79.

त्वं वेत्सि सर्वभूतानां पापानि सुकृतानि च।
व्यवहाराभिशस्तोष्यं मानवस्तुल्यते त्वया॥
देवासुरमनुष्याणां सत्ये त्वमतिरिच्यसे।
त्वं तुले सत्यधामासि पुरा देवैर्विनिर्मिता॥
तत्सत्यं वद कल्याणि संशयान्मां विमोचय।
यद्यहं पापकर्मास्मि तदा त्वं मामधो नय।

3. Yaj II

मुक्त्वाग्निं मृदितव्रीहिरदग्धः शुद्धिमाप्नुयात्।
अष्टेम मण्डले स्थित्वा नवमे मण्डलेऽग्नितप्तमयःपिण्डं त्यक्त्वा व्रीहीन् कराभ्यां मर्दयित्वाऽदग्धहस्तश्चेच्छुद्धिमाप्नुयात्। दग्ध हस्तश्चेदशुद्ध इत्यर्थसिद्धम्। यस्तु संत्रासात्प्रस्खलन्हस्ताभ्यामन्यत्र

दह्यते तथाप्यशुद्धो न भवति। यथाह कात्यायनः- 'प्रस्खलन्नभिशस्तश्चेत्स्थानादभ्यत्र दह्यते। अदग्धं तं विदुर्देवास्तस्य भूयोऽपि दापयेत्।इति॥

अन्तरा पतिते पिण्डे संदेहे वा पुनर्हरेत्॥

4. Narda IV.326.

शोधयैतं नरं पापात् सत्येनास्यामृती भव॥

छायानिवेशितो रक्ष्यो दिनशेषमभोजनः।

विषवेगकलमातीतः शुद्धोऽसौ मनुरब्रवीत्।

– शीर्षकस्थेऽभियोक्तरि

5. Yaj.II.95

6. Narda IV.257.

सव्रतानां भृशार्तानां व्याधितानां तपस्विनाम्।

स्त्रीणां च न भवेद्दिव्यं यदि धर्मस्त्ववेक्षते॥

शिरोवर्ती यदा न स्यात्तदा दिव्यं न दीयते।

कारणैः सहितं प्रोक्तं न दिव्यं चार्थिनान्नृणाम्॥

7. Yaj II.97

सचैलं स्नातमाहूय सूर्योदय उपोषितम्।

कारयेत्सर्वदिव्यानि नृपब्राह्मणसंनिधौ॥

Narda IV.268

सर्वदा स तु देयः स्यात् सर्वलोकस्य पश्यतः।

अहोरात्रोषिते स्नाते आर्द्रवाससि मानवे।

पूर्वाह्णे सर्वदिव्यानां प्रदानमनुकीर्त्तितम्।

शिरोपस्थायिनि नरे अभियोक्तयंपस्थिते।

8

Judges, Judging and Judgement

8

JUDGES, JUDGING AND JUDGEMENT

*

Appointment & Qualification of Judges, Judging of Cases, Pronouncement of Judgement

In vedic period, with neither any schools of law nor training nor any diploma or degree, the appointment of the judges was the prerogative of the king absolutely. However, the people well versed in Dharma Shastra & Vedic learning with clean and impeccable image, good family background and of restrained nature were chosen by the king for dispensing and administration of justice. An oral or written report in respect of a person being considered for appointment of judge was obtained through spies drafted by the king. Dharma did not mean faith or religion of a person but implies the knowledge of norms of conduct, polity and ethics on various matters mentioned in Dharmshastras e.g. vedas, smritis, shrutis, Dharma sutras and other such scriptures of Hindus.

Appointment of judges has always been the prerogative of the king. Manu says that, when owning to pressure of other weighty business, the king cannot attend to the work of administering justice and the king should appoint a learned *Brahman a* together with three *Sabhyas* to decide the disputes of people.[1] A major Rock Edict by Ashoka, the famous Mauryan ruler reads *"In the past there were no mahamatras responsible for the Dharma, but after a lapse of 13 years I have appointed Dharmamahamatras"*. This shows that the king was the appointing authority for the judges. However in a vast empire of Maurya rulers covering almost the whole India and borders flanking over a part of Afganistan, there have been thousands of courts each comprising of three judges, it was nay difficult for the king to appoint all the judges himself and therefore the administrative head of the respective Pradesh or region must have some autonomy in the matter of appointment of judges.

QUALIFICATION OF JUDGES

The qualification of a judge are set out in many places. The *Apasthamba Dhrama Sutra* prescribes that in lawsuits judges shall be endowed with learning, good family, and should be old, clever, and careful about *dharma.*[2] Narada required, "The Judge should be proficient in the texts on the eighteen titles of law, their eight thousand sub-heads, in logic and should be master of the *Veda* and *Smritis*, Katyayana says that a judge should be of restrained nature, born of a good family, impartial, not repellant (or harsh in his manners), steady afraid of the next world, assiduous and free from hot temper.

A judge was generally styled *pradvivaka* or *dharmadhyaksha* or *dharmapravaktr*[3] or *dharmadhikarin*. *Pradvivaka* is an ancient word. It occurs in *Gautama Smrti*[4] and *Narada Smrti.*[5] If a learned Brahmana cannot hold the post of the chief judge, then Kshatriya or Vaisya who knows dharmasastras may be appointed, but the king should carefully avoid appointing a Sudra as a judge. The king should appoint at least three[6] sabhyas (judges or members of the court of justice) to associate with the Chief Judge in the disposal of suits.

Sukranitisara and others however, required the following qualifications in the *Sabhyas* :

i) they should be endowed with the study of the *Vedas*,
ii) should know dharmasastra,
iii) should speak the truth,
iv) should be impartial to friend or foe,
v) should be steady devoted to their work,
vi) intelligent, hereditary, proficient in *arthasastra*.

DISQUALIFICATION

The king was not to appoint as *Sabhyas* those, who were ignorant of the usages of the country, who were atheists and devoid of the study of *sastras*, who were either puffed up, hot-tempered, greedy or distressed.

The learned Brahmanas were in the position of *amicus curiae*. All and sundry were not to intermeddle in trials before the court, but only those who were learned in *dharmasastra* were allowed to express their opinions on knotty points.[6] Katyayana makes it the duty of the *Sabhyas* to bring round a king gradually to the right path when the king is about to start on the path of injustice and to state the true decision. In the case of the Brahmanas their duty ends with stating the rule according to the *sastras;* they have not, like the *Sabhyas*, to prevent the king from doing the wrong thing or to bring him round to the path of right and justice.

Kautilya prescribes that the courts called *Dharmasthiya* should be manned by three judges called dharmasthas who should possess the qualifications and status of amatyas and that such courts should be established on the borders of the provinces, for a group of ten villages for a district, and provinces. Brhaspati says that the *sabhyas* may be seven, five or three. As in the case of the chief judge, the sabhyas should be preferably Brahmanas, but they may be Kshatriyas or Vaisyas.

CONSTITUENTS OF A COURT OF JUSTICE.

The *Sabha* is said to have ten *angas* by Brhaspati, they are :

1. The King
2. The Chief Judge appointed by the king
3. The Sabhyas
4. Smrti
5. Ganaka (accountant)
6. Lekhala (the scribe)
7. Gold
8. Fire
9. Water
10. Svapurusha / Sadhyapala (bailiff)

The chief judge declares the law, the king awards punishment, the *Sabhyas* examine the dispute, *Smrti* lays down the rule of decision, the success (of one party or the other) and the punishment; gold and fire are required for taking oaths, the water is for men when they feel thirsty, the *Ganaka* counts the wealth or subject matter of dispute, the scribe writes down the pleadings, depositions and the decision, the *Purusha* summons the *Sabhyas*, the defendant, the witnesses, and the guards, the complainant and the defendant when they have furnished no surety (for appearance).

JUDGING AND JUDGEMENT

A legal case would be judged according to the four basics of justice. These, in order of increasing importance, are:

1. Dharma, which is based on truth
2. Evidence, which is based on witness
3. Custom, i.e., the tradition accepted by the people
4. Royal Edicts, i.e., law promulgated

There shall be established a bench of three judges who shall hold court at frontier posts, sub-district quarters, and provincial headquarters. The judges shall be learned in dharma and have the qualifications of a minister. They shall judge (civil) cases arising from disputes between two parties. Judges shall be fined and removed from offices if they act against dharma. A bench of three magistrates (pradeshtr), each of the rank of minister, shall be responsible for the suppression of anti-social activities.

Narada requires that all the judges of the court should give a unanimous decision, and that then only the decision leaves no grievance (in the mind of the litigants). According to Gautama as interpreted by Apararka, if there is a difference of opinion among the judges, the king is to seek the advice of those who are learned in the three Vedas (along with other *vidyas*) and decide the matter finally.

The king should sit in his court to administer justice. The *Arthasastra* says "when in the court, the king shall never cause his petitioners to wait at the door".[6] *Amatyas* were appointed in the courts. The *Arthasastra* says that the "Amatyas (officers) purified by religious test, should be employed in civil and criminal courts. This shows that before appointment as judge, the ineumbent was subjected to a religions test and only there after he was sworn in as judge, as mentioned by Kautilya.

ACCOUNTABILITY OF JUDGES

The ancient preceptors were aware of the human weakness and frequent failure of a person to adhere to the expected level of conduct and moral values and to get tempted by the lust of wealth, sex, money or fame. The judges being the sons of the same soil, were no exception, as such they were to face penal action in case of dereliction of their duties or to act with extraneous or ulterier consideration or vested interest.

Naradasmriti says "If the sabhyas give a decision, which is opposed to smriti and usage, out of frendship, greed or feare, each was liable to be fined twice as much as the fine to be paid by the defeated party (Nar. 1.67). It was held that where an unjust decision is rendered, a quarter of the sin falls on the litigant (plaintiff or defendant) who is guilty of adharma, one quarter each on the witnesses, the sabhyas and the king".

Yajnavalka smriti also contians a similar provision in case a judge was found to act in violation of the prescribed norms of Dharma. There have been instances when the penal action was taken against judges (sabhyas) in case of any default on their part was proved.

REFERENCES

1. यदा स्व्यं न कुर्यात्तु नृपतिः कार्यदर्शनम्।
   तदा नियुज्याद्विद्वांसं ब्राह्मणं कार्यदर्शने॥
   सोऽस्य कार्याणि संपश्येत्सभ्यैरेव त्रिभिर्वृतः।
   सभामेव प्रविश्याग्रयामासीनः स्थित एव वा॥ - Manu VIII. 9-10.
2. धर्मशास्त्रार्थकुशलाः कुलीनाः सत्यवादिनः।
   समा शत्रौ च मित्र न नृपतेः स्युः सभासदः॥ - Narda III.5
3. जातिमात्रोपजीवी वा कामं स्याद् ब्राह्मणब्रुवः।
   धर्मप्रवक्ता नृपतेन्न तु शूद्रः कथंचन॥ - Manu VIII. 20.
4. Gaut III 26.27 and 31.
5. Narda 1.35
6. Manu VIII-9 and 10
7. यत्र सभ्यो जनः सर्वः साध्वेतदिति मन्यते।
   स निःशल्यो विवादः स्यात् सशल्यः स्यादतोऽन्यथा॥Narda III.17

8. उपस्थानगतः कार्यार्थिनामद्वारासङ्गं कारयेत्। दुर्दर्शो हि राजा कार्याकार्यविपर्यासमासन्नैः कार्यते। तेन प्रकृतिकोपमरिवशं वा गच्छेत्। तस्माद्देवताश्रमपाषण्डश्रोत्रियपशुपुण्यस्थानानां बालवृद्धव्याधित-व्यसन्यनाथानां स्त्रीणां च क्रमेण कार्याणि पश्येत्; कार्यगौरवादात्ययिकवशेन वा।

- Kautilya 1.1

9. तत्र धर्मोपधाशुद्धान् धर्मस्थीयकण्टकशोधनेषु स्थापयेत् अर्थोपधाशुद्धान् समाहर्तृसन्निधातृनिचयकर्मसु, कामोपधाशुद्धान् बाह्याभ्यन्तरविहारक्षासु, भयोपधाशुद्धानासन्नकार्येषु राज्ञः। सर्वोपधाशुद्धान् मन्त्रिणः कुर्यात्। सर्वत्राशुचीन् खनिद्रव्यहस्तिवनकर्मान्तेषूपयोजयेत्।

- Kautilya 1.3

9

Bar Code in Ancient India

9

BAR CODE IN ANCIENT INDIA

(My Lord - Your Honour)

*

In modern India judges are usually addressed as *'milord'* (mylord) or your *'lordship'* while hearing the legal cases in their court. The Bar Council of India has recently amended the wording of address as 'your honour' or 'honourable court'. Explaining the decision to drop the archaic and colonial prefix of 'Your Lordship' from the court rulebook, India's Chief Justice famously said, "The Lord is only one and he is God above all of us. I am not God, judges are not gods." Other countries i.e. U.S.A. the judges are addressed as 'your honour' and in some muslim countries like Saudi Arbia etc. the verbal address of judges is in pure arabic.

The designation of judicial posts in modern India vary according to level of the post, i.e. at metro level, district level, State level or National level. The designation of judges at the lowest echelon is magistrate (dealing with criminal cases) or sub-judge for civil cases, session judge / district judge at the district level. At state level courts i.e. High court, judges are addressed as justice and chief justice. Similarly at national level court, the judges are designated as justice and chief justice of that country.

In Ancient India a judge was generally addressed *pradvivaka* or *dharmapravaktr*[1] or *dharmadhikarin*. Pradvivaka is an ancient world. It occurs in Gautama smirti[2] and Narada smriti. During Mauryan period a judge was called as dharmastha upholder of Dharma. Pradeshtr (magistrates) were another class of judicial officers. The appointed person was associated with law and justice and would explain the Dharmashastra to the king.

A post with a designation of Dhamma-Mahamatra analogous to a Supreme Court judge in modern legal term was created by Ashoka thirteen years after his coronation as he states in Rock Edict V. which sets forth their duties in some detail. The Dhamma-Mahamatras were to establish and promote Dharma among all sects in the land. They reviewed all sentences awarded by courts and mitigated or remitted their hardship after taking into account the particular circumstances of each case.

The *Rajukas* also performed judicial duties. Asoka asked them to perform their duties confidently and fearlessly and desired that the care of these officers should resemble that of "an intelligent nurse for the child in her charge".

Nagala-Viyohalakas (Nagara Vyavaharikas) – They administered justice in the city, analygous to Metropolitan magistrates. The distinction between judges and magistrates, seems to be that, the former would deal with all cases concerning transactions between two parties. The latter were concerned with crimes against society in general. The magistrates also combined executive and judicial functions. Both judges and magistrates were subordinates of the samahatr, the chancellor. There, were benches of three judges or three magistrates.

As par Kautilay's Arthashatras, the civil and criminal courts should have judicial officers with the designation of amatyas; and dharmasthas (judges well-versed in the sacred law). Amatya was also the chief executive officer. A designation adhyakshas has been used for magistrates who had the charge of hunters and had the power of punishing the defaulters.

During Ashokan period and also other Mauryan kings, the special tribunals were comprised of three judges, designated as Vyavaharika, Mahamatras and Rajukas respectively. Ashoka conferred special powers to Mahamtyas to check maladministration and to mitigate hardship faced on account of strict judgement.

In post Gupta period, there is a reference of the term as dharmadhikarins (judges) who sat on high level seats. A designation of Pramatro also figures in post Gupta inscriptions.

Official designations of Judicial and Administrative Posts in Gupta Period:

1) Kumaramatya : it was a designation of a class of high ranking officers who served in various capacities. The legends found on the Basarh sealings mention Kumaramatya in various contexts. We also find that emperor Samudraguptas's minister of peace and war had the title Kumaramatya.
2) Sriranabhandagar : Department of Military Stores.
3) Dandaypasik – adhikaranasya : Officer in charge of the police.
4) Vinayasthiti sthapak-adhikaranasya : officer in charge of education and the maintenance of the established norm of life.
5) Mahapratihara : Chief Chamberlain.
6) Mahadandanayaka : a judge, magistrate or a leader of the army.
7) Uparika : Officer in charge of the bhukti

REFERENCES

1. Manu VIII.20
2. Gaut. III. 26.27 and 31.
3. तत्र धर्मोपधाशुद्धान् धर्मस्थीयकण्टकशोधनेषु स्थापयेत्, अर्थोपधाशुद्धान् समाहतृसन्निधातृनिचयकर्मसु, कामोपधाशुद्धान् बाह्याभ्यन्तर विहाररक्षासु, भयोपधाशुद्धानासन्नकार्येषु राज्ञः। सर्वोपधाशुद्धान् मन्त्रिणः कुर्यात्। सर्वत्राशुचीन् खनिद्रव्यहस्तिवनकर्मान्तेषूपयोजयेत्।

- Kautilaya 1.5.3.

* H.T. News

10

Schools of Law Education in Ancient India

10

SCHOOLS OF LAW EDUCATION IN ANCIENT INDIA

Vedas are the most ancient scriptures of Hinduism and are regarded as the fountain head of all learnings even sciences. In due course of time the learning of Vedas became more and more obscure and the deep meaning and high philosophical thinking yoked with the hymns of Vedas was beyond the reach of comprehension of ordinary people. Followed by *Brahmnas* & Upnishdas more than 200 in number, the massive and varied literature created an intellectual confusion also. As such there was a need of simplified literature as well as clear guidance & directions to be imparted in simple language Smrities as well as dharm sutras was the result of the necessity. They contain ordains and regulations on varied matters of life, like birth, education, marriage, divorce, the rituals and *vavharas* and the daily conduct of people.

The smritis provide the directions and advice on various aspect of law and judicial system, like kinds of Apradhas, (crimes and guilt) their disposal, filing of plaints, hearing of cases composition and setup of a court, qualification and appointment of judges, pronouncement of judgement etc.

It needs to be clarified that the smritikars were not vested with any power of enforcement of the ordains and directions mentioned in simirities, which was the sole prerogative of a king of soveriegn state as to what extent he could follow the guidance provided by similites in legal and judicial matters. Every kingdom had its own penal code. The smritikars were no law makers but were the exponents of divine precept of law on the basis of earlier scriptures and they claimed no originality.

Growth and Development of Schools of Law

With teacher's home as school in Vedic period, there were small vedic schools run by acharyas and prreptors mostly Brhammas, imparting education in Vedic learning. The number of the students would be small according to the accomodation available in the home of the teacher. Charnas, Kulas, Shrenis etc were also the kinds of schools. The curriculum of study was the text of Vedas, Vedangas comprising of kathas, Niruktas etc. which were to be committed to memory with recitation and appropriate phoneology. In course of time, subsidiary subjects i.e. Angas, the rituals, grammar phonics etc were added with the curriculum to respond the need of the time. And thereafter sacred law as a seperate subject was also added with each vedic school having subject contents on Dharma. Thus sacred Hindu law has its origin in vedic schools which was basically meant to teach duties to the students of the school.

Ashrma Institutes

During Epic period as mentioned in Maha bharta, big asharmas/ hermitages were set up by renowned sages and preceptors having teaching faculty in various angas and specialties like Astronomy, Kalpas, Angas etc. Description of Kanva Ashram as given in Maha bharta reads, as under which was situated on the banks of Malini – a tributary river.

"The entire forest was full of hearths where sacred fire was burning, and resounding with the chanting or recitation of sacred texts by learned Brahmins. The wide range and variety of their studies is also indicated. There was specialties in every branch of learning cultivated in that

age; specialists in each of the four Vedas; in sacrificial literature and art; Kalpa-Sutras; in the art of reciting the Samhitas according to the Pada and Krama patha, and in Orthoepy generally, and in Siksha (Phonetics), Chhanda (Metrics), Sabda (Vyakarana), and Nirukta. There were also the philosophers well versed in Atma-Vijnana (Science of the Absolute), in Brahmopasana (Worship of Brahma), in Mokshadharma (the way to salvation), and in Lokayata (Vaiseshika). There were also Logicians knowing the principles of Nyaya, and of Dialectics (the art of establishing propositions, solving doubts, and ascertaining conclusions). There were also specialists in the physical sciences and arts. There were, for example, experts in the art of constructing sacrificial altars of various dimensions and shapes (on the basis of a knowledge of Solid Geometry); those who had knowledge of the properties of matter (dravyaguna); of physical processes and their results, of causes and their effects; and zoologists having a special knowledge of monkeys and birds.

Such a big set up is well comparable to a kind of forest universaty. During Sutra Period 600 B.C to 300 B.C., which was a period of specialization & scientific research, the contents of vedic education to which were added angas of vedas began to develop, and were made entirely independent of vedic studies, giving birth to special Law schools. As a result of this spell sacred law had also to part company from vedic schools resulting into setting up separate law schools. These schools offered the study material given in various, smirites and Dharm Sastres; Subsequently they composed their own secondary manual and secondary smirities.

Process of Development

The process of development of 'sacred law' as a separate subject appears to have started even earlier than Panini - the famous grammarian. The use of the word as '*Dharm Vidya*' which means the Science of sacred Law, speaks clearly in this regard. During the period of Panini and Maurya rulers specialists in Nyaya, Mimansa Nirukta and law acquired an important place in society as well as an Parishads - the Vedic institutions of higher order. Schools of law produced new dharmasastras, one of which is ascribed to the Upanishadic sage Yajanavalkya, which formed the basis of the Hindu family law in most of India until it was supplanted by legislation in the 1950s. In Buddhism, the Yogachara school emerged, the starting point of many developments in the Buddhism of later times in India, Tibet and China.

The law schools of the Gupta Age developed new rules about slavery as it existed in the preceding period. Adultery ranking among the lesser sins which should be expiated by the performance of appropriate penances. Only in extreme cases, and as when a woman commits adultery with a Sudra or other low caste man, or has conceived or borne a child, or attempts to kill her husband, she is to be abandoned altogether.

The other prominent names of schools of law of ancient India were Mitakshara and Dayabhag a Bangali School. The Mitabshara was functioning at Beuaras in Uttar Pradesh. With the passage of time, the king made laws grew more & more superior superseding the sacred law. Infact simiritis admit that the king is the supreme authority in matters of law. Narda Smiriti says :

"Gatherings (Kula), Corporations (Sreṇi), Assemblies (Gana), one appointed (by the king) and the King himself, are vested with the power to decide law suits; and of these, each succeeding one is superior to the one proceeding in order.

During the days of Hindu decline, the king made laws over-shadowed the smiriti law - much more in criminal cases and the own penal code of kingdom was ruling the roost.

BIBLIOGRAPHY

1. Ancient Indian Education, R.K. Mukherji.
2. Naradasmiriti.
3. Introduction to the laws of Manu, sacred books of the East series Vol. 23.
4. Mulla, D.F., Principles of Hindu Law.

11

Jail Bail and Warrant

11

JAIL BAIL AND WARRANT

Under modern judicial system the defendent or the accused of a crime is summoned to the court of law by issuing summon or warrant which is served in person to be present in the court on specific date and time. Also arrest is made after registering FIR when a prima facia is made out against the accused for commiting an offence. The accused is released on bail later on after having furnished personal or financial surety as decided by the court.

In ancient India samritis have prescribed detailed rules for summoning the defendent to the court and also for arrest or restairing the accused person. Narda smriti has laid down following rules in this regard.

Summoning of Accused / Defendent

Narada (I. 52-54) prescribed that cowherds when it is the season for taking cows for grazing, agriculturists in the sowing season, artisans actually engaged in work and soldiers engaged in war should not be summoned to appear in person, while so engaged. In these cases some one on their behalf should be summoned as a representative. But it is provided that even these persons may be summoned with proper safeguards in important cases or grave charges, such as the killing of human beings, theft, rape, eating forbidden food, counterfeiting coins, high treason, etc.

In the case of those who are exempted from personal appearance their relatives or some other person appointed by them or one who can be recognized as their agent may be allowed to appear. However, according to Narada, if a person who is not a brother nor father nor son nor appointed to represent another prosecutes a law-suit for another, he is liable to be fined.

The plaintiff may put under restraint till the approach of the bailiff by the king's order. A defendant would not be liable to be fined, if he disregards a restraint order which ties him down to a river bed, or to a forest, to a bad place (infested by thieves and tigers) or at the time of an invasion (Narada I. 49).

REFERENCES

1. स्थानासेधः कालकृतः प्रवासात्कम्रणस्तथा।
चतुर्विधः स्यादासेधो नासिद्धस्तं विलङ्येत्।।48।।
नदीसन्तारकान्तारदुर्देशोपप्लवलादिषु।
आसिद्धस्तं परासेधमुत्क्रामन्नापराध्नुयात्।।49।।
राजप्रतयक्षदृष्टानि सुहृत्संबन्धिबान्धवैः।
प्राप्तद्विगुणदण्डानि कार्याणि पुनरुद्धरेत्।।50।।
'आसेधकाल आसिद्ध आसधं यो व्यतिक्रमेत्।
स विनेयोऽन्यथा कुर्वन्नासेधा दण्डभाग् भवेत्।।51।।
निर्वेष्टुकामो रोगार्त्तो यियक्षु र्व्यसनेस्थितः।
अभियुक्तस्तथान्येन राजकार्योद्यतस्तथा।।52।।
गवां प्रचारे गोपालाः शस्यारम्भे कृषोबलाः।
शिल्पनश्चापि तत्कालमायुधोयाश्च विग्रहे।।53।।
अप्राप्तव्यवहारश्च दूतो दानोन्मुखो व्रती।
विषमस्थश्च नासेध्यो न चैतानाह्वयेन्नृपः।।54।।
नाभियुक्तोऽभियुञ्जीत तमतीत्वार्थमन्यतः।
न चाभियुक्तमन्येन न विद्धं वेद्धमर्हति।।55।।

- Narda 1, 52-54.